A Passage to Peace

Nur Yalman is Professor of Social Anthropology and Middle Eastern Studies at Harvard University. A Fellow of the American Academy of Arts and Sciences, his major work is the classic anthropological text *Under the Bo Tree: Studies in Caste, Kinship and Marriage in the Interior of Ceylon* (1967). He works across the fields of religion and politics in South Asian, Central Asian, Middle Eastern and other Muslim societies, and has conducted ethnographic fieldwork in Sri Lanka, India, Iran and Turkey.

Daisaku Ikeda is President of Soka Gakkai International, a Buddhist organization with some twelve million adherents in over 192 countries and regions throughout the world. He is the author of over 80 books on Buddhist themes, and received the United Nations Peace Award in 1993. His work to restore Chinese–Japanese relations as well as his contributions to world peace, cultural exchange and education have been widely recognized. The world's academic community has awarded him more than 240 academic degrees.

A Passage to Peace
Global Solutions from
East and West

Nur Yalman and
Daisaku Ikeda

I.B. TAURIS
LONDON · NEW YORK

Published in 2009 by I.B.Tauris & Co Ltd
6 Salem Road, London W2 4BU
175 Fifth Avenue, New York NY 10010
www.ibtauris.com

In the United States of America and Canada
distributed by Palgrave Macmillan, a division of St Martin's Press
175 Fifth Avenue, New York NY 10010

Appendix 2 is published by permission of the Transnational Foundation for
Peace and Future Research, Sweden

ISBN (HB) 978 1 84511 922 5
ISBN (PB) 978 1 84511 923 2

A full CIP record for this book is available from the British Library
A full CIP record is available from the Library of Congress

Library of Congress Catalog Card Number: available

Typeset by JCS Publishing Services Ltd, www.jcs-publishing.co.uk
Printed and bound in Great Britain by TJ International Ltd, Padstow, Cornwall

Contents

Preface by Nur Yalman   vii

Preface by Daisaku Ikeda   ix

One   Cultural Resonances   1

Two   Loyalty to All Humanity   19

Three   Peace Within and Without   33

Four   Mutual Understanding for a Better World   47

Five   Intercultural Communion   61

Six   Empathy and Our Shared Humanity   73

Seven   Reviving Asian Humanism   85

Eight   Global Governance   99

Nine   Dialogue: the Magna Carta of Civilization   109

Ten   New Paths for Education   119

Appendix 1   The Kemalist Revolution: A Model
by Daisaku Ikeda   131

Appendix 2 Terror and Cultural Diversity in Times of
           Adversity by Nur Yalman   141

           Glossary   157
           Notes   169
           Index   173

Preface by Nur Yalman

This is a volume of conversations about the world views (*Weltanschauung*) of two great nations situated at opposite ends of the vast continent of Asia. Japan is an astonishing, unique land that has caught the imagination of scholars, writers and artists, not to mention politicians and soldiers, for the last two centuries in the West. Similarly, Turkey, at the western end of Asia, was at the heart of a vast empire bringing together peoples and cultures from Russia and the Balkans, to the ancient lands of Syria, Iraq, Egypt and Arabia – all the way from the Caucasus to Algeria.

Both Japanese and Turks have profoundly affected the course of events in history. Both have been demonized at different times by the great powers. I am grateful to Mr Daisaku Ikeda for providing me with the opportunity to address the Japanese people, who are so much admired in Turkey.

As you will read in these discussions, there is much that brings Japan and Turkey together at this moment in history. They have played similar roles as champions of Asia in confronting the great powers. They are now both part of a larger picture of free nations with progressive, open political systems that have so much to offer to the rest of humanity.

Because of my personal passion for the great civilizations of Asia, and as a social anthropologist with deep interest in Sri Lanka, we also discuss modern trends in the social sciences.

If the ills of hunger, inequality, oppression, ignorance and violence that affect many peoples are to be addressed, we must be aware of the accomplishments in the liberal social sciences in the last fifty years. Social anthropology, with its emphasis on 'understanding', has played a vital role in the interpretation and understanding of other cultures. In this respect, I must express my admiration for Mr Ikeda for his extraordinary insight into the intimate details of Turkish life, history, customs and beliefs.

Buddhism and Islam have had an intimate history through ancient contacts in Central Asia and India. Even though turbulent at times, there is no doubting the profound influence of Buddhist thought and practice on key institutions of Islam – Sufism, the emphasis on the simple life, dervishes and otherworldliness come to mind. Japan has certainly had brilliant interpreters and writers on Islam. At this time, when the powerful symbols of religious commitment are being used by unscrupulous persons for nefarious ends, it is all the more important to bring those universal values of humanity, sincerity, simplicity and empathy, which are so much at the core of both Buddhism and Islam, to the public. Japan and Turkey must be pioneers in this aspect as well.

Nur Yalman, Istanbul

Preface by Daisaku Ikeda

The seas do not separate us; rather, they bring us closer together. I first visited Istanbul, the ancient capital of Turkey, in 1962. It was a deeply moving experience for me. To the north lay Russia and the home of the Slavic peoples; to the south, the broad expanse of the Mediterranean and the continent of Africa. Here the civilization of ancient Greece flourished; this, in the time of the Byzantine Empire, was the centre of the world of Eastern Christianity; and here, under the Ottoman Empire, Islamic culture flowered into greatness. It is a crossroads, a meeting place of many cultures and civilizations.

Looking down on the Bosporus, I could see the numerous vessels threading their way back and forth across the blue sea. The distance from one shore to the other is about one kilometre. Between these two shores, at this strategic point in the Eurasian continent – this boundary between Europe and Asia, this place where so many different peoples have lived side by side – here the sea shines in peaceful and radiant beauty.

I first met the world-renowned cultural anthropologist Dr Nur Yalman (a native of Istanbul) in March 1992, just before I made my second visit to Turkey. I was particularly struck by his wonderful smile, like a fresh sea breeze that could not fail to warm the heart of anyone who encountered it, though whether this was a feature of his innate nature, or something he had acquired in the course of his long years of fieldwork in anthropology, I had no way of knowing.

At the present time, when our communications networks have reached such an advanced stage of development, why is it that we seem to make so little progress in matters of mutual understanding? This is a question of deep concern to Dr Yalman. He has aptly defined his speciality, that of cultural anthropology, as 'an attempt to understand other people'. I heartily admire and agree with that definition. For here, if ever there was one, is a study that humankind urgently needs today.

Dr Yalman, whose aim is to deal with the aporia or difficult problems confronting the world today, has stated:

> Claude Lévi-Strauss, a pioneer in the field of cultural anthropology, has said, 'We must bend our ears to hear the sound of the wheat growing. With great care, and exerting all our efforts, we must do our best to understand and nourish the diversity of human beings.' By this he meant that we must create a tolerant culture that recognizes this diversity and respects the rights of minorities.

On the basis of these convictions, Dr Yalman has demonstrated a profound understanding of Islamic society; he has also carried out fieldwork studies based upon a survey of Buddhism in Sri Lanka. By casting light on the richness and diversity that characterize different cultures, he has opened avenues by which various groups of human beings may communicate with one another.

In September 1993, I received an invitation from the Department of Anthropology at Harvard University, of which Dr Yalman was then the head, to give a lecture – the second such invitation I had received from Harvard. My lecture, entitled 'Mahayana Buddhism and Twenty-First-Century Civilization', was intended in part as a reply to questions raised by Dr Yalman through his recent studies. The day following the lecture, Dr Yalman kindly invited me to his home. The hours we spent in his lush garden discussing environmental problems and the great civilizations of the past, with the sunlight filtering down on us through the branches of the autumn trees, are among my most treasured memories.

Since then, Dr Yalman has lent his unstinting support and cooperation in matters pertaining to the Boston Research Center for the 21st Century, an organization for peace studies that I founded, as well as contributing to the activities of the Toda Institute for Global Peace and Policy Research. I would like to take this opportunity to once again express my sincere thanks for the kindness he has shown in this respect over many years.

Time has passed, and now, in the world of the twenty-first century we are faced by growing tension with the threat of terrorism and the proliferation of nuclear arms. In addition, environmental concerns such as those associated with global warming and the ever-increasing problem of poverty cast dark shadows over the future of the human race. We must awaken to the fact that such problems can no longer be regarded with indifference. They must be confronted through the power of dialogue and education, designed to unite the hearts of all individuals. The time has come for a united effort by all humanity – an effort that must transcend all differences of race and nationality, religion and culture.

This volume represents a collection of dialogues in which Dr Yalman and I have sought to crystallize our mutually held beliefs. Through the medium of dialogue, we have endeavoured to create a bridge that will serve to connect the two civilizations of Islam and Buddhism.

At present there are some 1.3 billion people living within the sphere of Islamic civilization, approximately one-fifth of the total population of the globe. Among these individuals are many who are my personal friends, all of them prized partners in peace, lovers of humanity, upholders of equality and advocates of tolerance. It is an urgent necessity for all of us to learn more about Islam and to deepen the understanding that exists between our worlds, for ignorance can only lead to greater hatred and tension. As a Buddhist text states, 'When that is done, then both oneself and others will take joy in their possession of wisdom and compassion.' No country, no race of people, must be left to exist in isolation. The path to dialogue must never be closed off. This is a lesson I learned from my mentor Josei Toda, the second president of Soka Gakkai.

In order to overcome the prejudices and misconceptions that abound in the world today, we must encourage a sense of empathy and mutual understanding among all human beings. This is the purpose that directs these dialogues between Dr Yalman and me. 'Empathy is the hallmark of true humanity.' 'It must be developed and can only evolve through person-to-person exchanges.' These are Dr Yalman's own words, words that strike my heart with a deep and unforgettable resonance.

There are at present two bridges spanning the Bosporus. And work is now in progress on a third link, the Marmara Project – Railway Bosporus Tube Passage – due to be completed around 2009.

Once a bridge has been built, the way is open for unlimited numbers of people to pass back and forth over it. Therefore, whenever warfare breaks out, the bridges are the first targets for attack. Bridges, you might say, are in fact symbols of peace.

In a world marked by deepening division and confrontation, the type of dialogues that transcend people's individual differences and bring them together as fellow human beings serve as bridges – connecting heart to heart and mind to mind. If the present volume of dialogues helps to suggest to the young people who will be the leaders of the future ways in which they might go about building a great cultural bridge that will tie together all humanity, then I could wish for no greater satisfaction.

Daisaku Ikeda, Tokyo

ONE

Cultural Resonances

The spirit of global citizenship

Ikeda: 'The world to me is sustenance,
    Its peoples and my own are one.'[1]

I concluded a speech I delivered at Ankara University in June 1992 with these inspiring words of the great thirteenth-century humanist Turkish poet Yunus Emre. Today, as rampant ethnic and religious conflict and discord cause untold misery, the spirit of global citizenship illuminating Emre's words shine brighter than ever.

Turkey, the land of your birth and upbringing, has a long tradition of amity and tolerance. With that background, as one of the most outstanding cultural anthropologists in the United States, you are promoting harmony among diverse peoples. I am extremely happy to have this opportunity to engage in dialogue with you to try to further the future of humanity and peace.

Yalman: I consider it an honour to be able to discuss matters with someone who is not only an outstanding Buddhist leader, philosopher, author and educator but also the brilliant head of Soka Gakkai International.

Ikeda: As head of the department of cultural anthropology, you were kind enough to invite me to lecture for a second time at Harvard University in September 1993. The title of my talk was 'Mahayana Buddhism and Twenty-First-Century Civilization'. The day after my lecture, you invited me to your home in Cambridge, Massachusetts. The autumn foliage was at its most beautiful, and I shall never forget the talks we had then.

Yalman: You devote immense effort to international dialogue for the promotion of mutual understanding and the formation of ties among diverse racial and ethnic groups. For example, you have encouraged exchanges between China and Japan, helping to build a bridge of amity between the two countries.

In this important and critical period for humanity, when there is much unwarranted talk of clashes of civilizations, I hope your influence will spread beyond Japan to reach the whole world. The attainment of peace and mutual understanding for the human race is obviously your cherished desire. It is mine as well. Contributing to peace now is my own long-standing wish and hope.

Ikeda: You are thoroughly familiar with world cultures. Of course, as a Turk, you know everything about Islam. In addition, I was astonished to learn during our three discussions how broad and profound your knowledge of Japanese culture and understanding of Buddhism are.

Yalman: And in turn I am greatly impressed with your extensive knowledge of Turkish history and tradition.

Istanbul – where East and West meet

Ikeda: Of all the fifty-four different countries I have visited, it is Turkey, on my two visits there – once in 1962 and again in 1992 – that has made an especially great impression on me.

Looking out over the Bosporus from my hotel in Istanbul, I experienced the city as the boundary between Asia and Europe – the place where Eastern and Western cultures come together. The experience was deeply moving.

Yalman: Although I live in the United States now, I go back to Turkey several times each year to assist in the development of new universities and to spend some time with friends and family. I have a special love for Istanbul, where I was born and grew up.

Ikeda: Walking around Istanbul's old quarter, you encounter architectural wonders everywhere. The eye-catching great dome and minarets of Suleiman's Mosque, for instance, reveal the might of the sultan it was named after.

Yalman: Yes. Not long ago, as I walked through the old part of town, I was struck afresh by the charm of the unbelievable magnificence of the dome and the skywards-pointing towers. When buildings like that are illuminated against the calm winter sky, I feel that Istanbul is the most exotic city in the world. Perhaps only Bangkok can compare with it. Tokyo is beautiful too, but it lacks the historical, mysterious qualities of Istanbul.

Ikeda: On all sides, one encounters a cultural melding of Persian, Arabian, Mongol, Greek, Russian, Balkan and East-European elements. Reputedly the most beautiful in the world, the sunsets are indeed unforgettable.

Bangkok is a wonderfully appealing city. I have been there many times and on three occasions have visited the Chitralada Palace to pay my respects to King Bhumibol Adulyadej.

Tokyo is a classic example of the sameness of modern cities. In Istanbul, on the other hand, traces of diverse cultures overlap like arabesques. With its great dome and minarets, the Hagia Sophia was originally built as the Christian Church of the Holy Wisdom of God, later converted into a mosque and is now the Aya Sophya Museum. Next to it is the great Hagia Irene, the temple to peace, situated in the courtyard of the Topkapi Palace, which houses treasures from all over the world. Other places of interest include the Grand Bazaar with its labyrinth of thousands of shops, the sarcophagus of Alexander the Great, and fortifications and columns from the age of the Roman Empire.

Yalman: Istanbul is highly diverse because it was the capital of three great empires: Roman, Byzantine and Ottoman. Historical sites abound everywhere.

Ikeda: Coffee drinking, originated by the Arabs, reached Europe and the rest of the world from Istanbul, where the first coffee shop opened in the sixteenth century. Turkish cuisine ranks with French and Chinese as some of the finest in the world.

Yalman: Because Turkish food is very complex, Turks consider it the great cuisine, superior to French and Chinese food. It is the result of long centuries of imperial culture, along with the combined traditions of the Mediterranean, Middle East and Caucasia.

Spiritual siblings

Ikeda: We Japanese have a fondness for and affinity with Turkey. The Turkish flag is a white crescent and star on a red ground. As if to complement it, the Japanese flag is a red sun on a white ground. Turkey is at the western end and Japan at the eastern end of the Silk Road. On my two visits to Turkey, I came to feel that, although we are separated by great geographical distances, we are spiritually close. Indeed, according to one theory, we are sibling peoples descended from one ethnic source.

Yalman: A historic relationship may indeed have existed between our two peoples.

Ikeda: I understand there is a Turkish legend to the effect that, long ago, in the very centre of the Eurasian continent there was a pure river, surrounded by beautiful hills, with green plains along its banks where people lived in harmony. At one point in history, oppressed by enemies, some of these people moved farther and farther eastward and crossed a sea. Others moved westward – to the remotest place from which the sea is visible. One group was the Japanese; the other, the Turks.

Yalman: That may have been, because the two peoples have very similar customs. They speak structurally similar languages – probably Altaic. They both sit on cushions on the floor and employ wrapping cloths – called *furoshiki* in Japanese and *bohcha* in Turkish.

Ikeda: Another story suggests a further similarity between us. Once Tughril Beg (c.993–1063), founder of the Turkish Seljuk Empire, assembled his family and asked one member to break an arrow. This the family member did easily. Tughril Beg then asked him to break two together, then three together. This he did but then proved incapable of breaking four arrows held in a bunch. Tughril Beg used the arrows as a symbol of the need for tribes to stick together. A similar Japanese story is told about a member of the warrior class named Mōri Motonari (1497–1571). In the Japanese version, it was three arrows that could not be broken.

Yalman: I am surprised to learn that Japan has a tale like that of Tughril Beg.

Ikeda: The year 2003 was designated the 'Year of Turkey' in Japan. A series of celebrations and exchange events continued until May 2004. In connection with this project, the Min-On Concert Association, which I founded, invited groups of

Turkish musicians and folk groups to perform. However, even before these events we worked to deepen friendship between our countries in the fields of culture and education. I hope this dialogue will provide an occasion for continuing those efforts.

Yalman: One of the significant outcomes of our unusual dialogue is the good opportunity it provides for introducing Turkish and Islamic cultures into Japan.

Ikeda: And that is an excellent thing because, unfortunately, very few people in Japan correctly understand the worlds of Turkey and Islam. Tsunesaburo Makiguchi, first president of Soka Gakkai, cautioned against judging things we know nothing about. That is why I want to start our dialogue in a way that will help our peoples get to know each other better.

The thirteenth-century Persian Sufi poet, Jalal al-Din Rumi (1207–73), said that exchanging even one word of understanding is wonderful, but being of one heart is far more wonderful. Because mutual understanding is the key to peace in the twenty-first century, we must all strive to know each other, be friends, and operate on the same mental wavelength. Friendship helps us appreciate each other's merits. Mutual trust evolves from broad reciprocal learning.

Yalman: Yes, and to do this we must create a culture that not only tolerates but also understands diversity and minorities. Unless understanding and mutual respect permeate society, from the masses to the national leaders, the twenty-first cannot be a century of peace.

Ikeda: That reminds me of something the great English historian Arnold J. Toynbee said. In his youth, he visited Turkey and wrote a report to an English newspaper about how Europeans were massacring Turks. To the torrent of criticism this produced, he replied, '. . . for all but a very small minority of my countrymen, the Turks were anonymous ogres . . . Turks had a pejorative collective label but no human personal names or countenances.'[2] He also emphasized the importance of friendship at the individual level because human beings are not inclined to commit atrocities on fellow human beings with whom they are personally acquainted.[3]

Lack of respect for cultural differences has caused many of the world's tragedies. This is why cultural exchanges at the level of the ordinary people are essential if we are to take pride in our differences, help diversity blossom and create positive values. This is another reason for working hard on this dialogue. Aside from that, however, I am eager to learn more about the daily lives of the Turkish people.

Yalman: I see. Well, please ask whatever you like. I shall be happy to answer.

Floral preferences

Ikeda: First, then, the blossoming cherry tree symbolizes Japan. What flower is representative of Turkey?

Yalman: I am delighted that your first question is about flowers. The Turks especially love carnations, roses and tulips.

Ikeda: They are popular in Japan, too.

Yalman: Roses are particularly associated with poetry – traditionally, Turkish and Persian poets have written of the love affair between nightingales and roses – a metaphor for the relationship between the lover and his beloved, and often for the relationship between man and God.

Ikeda: The metaphor has a religious as well as a romantic association.

Yalman: Yes. I have noticed that in my garden in Istanbul big roses bloom just at the time when nightingales are calling their mates for the spring rituals of lovemaking. So it is not surprising that poets hit upon the very attractive combination of nightingales and roses.

Ikeda: I understand that the Turks improved tulips through selective breeding and introduced them into Europe.

Yalman: Apparently the tulip was originally a wild flower in the Turkish mountains. At one point, the Turks went absolutely mad for them. Single tulip bulbs fetched immense prices. When the flowers were introduced into Holland in the sixteenth century, the Dutch too lost their heads over them – in Amsterdam in the seventeenth century, single bulbs sold for as much as a whole house.

Ikeda: Alexandre Dumas describes this madness in *La Tulipe Noire*, which deals with the tremendously expensive attempts to cultivate the fabulous black tulip. A spark from this craze ignited in Turkey as well.

Yalman: A whole period of Ottoman history associated with tulips is referred to as the 'Tulip Age'. In their gardens, important politicians and rich people used small tortoises with candles placed on their backs to illuminate tulips in charming settings, where poets sang and musicians performed.

Unfortunately, this kind of extravagance caused popular revolts. Ultimately, the Ottoman state was pretty well bankrupted by such excesses. But it was a period associated with flowers – the poets and the musicians must have had fun while it lasted.

Lively tradition of popular literature

Ikeda: To move on to another topic: what kind of literature is most popular in Turkey?

Yalman: Turkey has a very lively tradition of popular literature. Among the important writers are Yaşar Kemal and Orhan Pamuk.

Ikeda: Yaşar Kemal has been nominated for the Nobel Prize on several occasions.

Yalman: That is true. We are delighted that Orhan Pamuk has now been honoured with the Nobel Prize at last. This is a recognition of the immense history and richness of the literature of the Turks. I should like to mention also the great poet Nazim Hikmet.

Ikeda: In his poem 'The Dead Little Girl', a child who died in the atomic bombing of Hiroshima requests people to petition against war and in favour of peace. It is very well known in Japan and has even been set to music. It contains these lines:

> I am knocking at your doors,
> aunts and uncles, to get your signatures
> so that never again children will burn
> and so they can eat sweets.

Yalman: Though he produced magnificent poetry, Hikmet was controversial because he was a Communist. Some people in Turkey think he was a traitor, but most appreciate his poetry. He was among the great writers and thinkers who have significantly affected Turkey.

Ikeda: What Turkish classics would you say correspond to Japanese poetry anthologies like the *Man'yōshū* (Collection of Ten Thousand Leaves) and the *Kokin Wakashū* (Collected Japanese Poems from Ancient and Modern Times)?

Yalman: Perhaps the tradition of religious poetry – including the work of Islamic mystics such as Rumi, Yunus Emre and numerous other poets.

Ikeda: And the Koran.

Yalman: Of course, the Koran is recited extensively. Interestingly, the Koran is written in very special, classical Arabic that is different from the language spoken day to day in Arab countries. It is rather like the Latin used in the Catholic Church. The Koran is a special kind of literature, unlike popular novels.

Women in society

Ikeda: I understand. Now, I should like to ask you something that interests many of our readers. When did the custom of veiling women's faces start?

Yalman: I understand that it probably antedates Islam. Aristocratic women of ancient Persia and Rome covered their heads – they were considered too special for ordinary people to look upon. For a long time, the difference between Islam and Christianity was not very great in this respect, since European women also covered their heads.

Ikeda: It is not, then, a custom specific to Islam.

Yalman: No. However, things changed drastically in Europe with the nineteenth-century emancipation of women. In the Islamic world, the tradition of the veil has been preserved. It took a great deal of time for people to realize that veiling women does not go well with a modern way of life. It gives the impression, whether accurate or not, that women must be protected – by men.

Ikeda: What is the situation in Turkey?

Yalman: Due to the efforts of modernizers, the veil was eliminated in Turkey for a long period of time. Surprisingly, however, in recent elections a party vigorously supporting the veiling of women and other traditional Islamic practices has come into political power. We shall see whether they continue the practice of veiling women or begin to modernize and follow the rest of the developed world in allowing women the freedom to decide how they want to express themselves.

Ikeda: That will be most interesting.

Yalman: Veiling is a demonstration of the idea that, as special, even sacred people, women need to be protected. This ancient concept regrettably led to traditional subjugation of women and relegation of them to the status of second-rate individuals subject to masculine control. We see a lot of this all over Asia and indeed all over the world, wherever men dominate women. This is changing, but only slowly – even in Japan.

Ikeda: Undeniably, in the past men have dominated many aspects of Japanese society. But ultimately unilateral masculine dominance is sure to reach an impasse. A society can only truly prosper if it respects women's opinions, learns from their wisdom and affords them maximum respect.

Yalman: The issue is related to the kind of world we are developing in the twenty-first century. My own belief is that, inevitably, in the developed world, with more women in the workforce, the sexes will become more and more equal in every respect. As this happens, symbols indicating female subjugation will fade away.

Ikeda: I think this will – must – happen. For some time, I have been saying that the twenty-first must be the century for women.

Yalman: The question is whether, given the duties of childbirth and upbringing, absolute equality of the sexes is possible. That is not an easy question to answer. The role of the family and the role of women within the family are going to continue to be debated with ever-increasing significance all over the world. In many Western countries, as combining the obligations of home and workplace becomes too difficult, large numbers of women elect not to have children.

In the marketplace

Ikeda: The custom of setting no fixed prices in the souks and bazaars of Islamic countries seems odd to people accustomed to fast-food stores selling the same product for the same price everywhere. From the opposite viewpoint, however, setting a standard price in a satellite office in some distant country seems just as odd.

Yalman: Universal pricing is one of the negative aspects of globalization. Allowing sellers to adjust prices to the customer is a more pleasant way of doing business.

Ikeda: Yes, because in addition to purely economic considerations, such as material costs and transport, a human element comes into play in price setting.

In Osaka, a city of which I am very fond, merchants and customers bargain together over prices. A skilful customer can talk a price way down. What is more, both sides enjoy themselves tremendously. When he thinks he has come down as much as he can, the seller grimaces and says something like, 'All right, I'll take the loss!'

Some people think that the Japanese term *benkyo-suru* (to study), which is also used to mean 'to offer a discount', indicates how the seller actually learns from communicating with the purchaser. Be that as it may, in such negotiations elements of human advantage and exchange are added to considerations of mere economic advantage. Probably the same kind of thing applies to negotiations in souks and bazaars.

Yalman: The fixed prices of modern commerce standardize human relations that are essentially diverse.

Ikeda: There are those who interpret the lack of fixed prices at souks and bazaars as outdated and economically inefficient. But surely the souk system deserves praise for enriching human relationships in daily life.

Our current age of global communication requires deeper mutual understanding. In this connection, your own work in cultural-anthropological efforts to understand other people is of increasing importance. In a broad sense, yours is the viewpoint of the ordinary people and their ways of life in numerous diverse cultures. Our dialogue has convinced me how important a strong viewpoint of the people is to humanity.

Festivals and funerals

Ikeda: Now to turn to the question of festivals. Everybody in Japan celebrates the New Year. Do you have any Turkish festivals in which everybody in the country takes part?

Yalman: Major Turkish festivals are associated with the Islamic religion: celebrations at the end of Ramadan, the Hajj pilgrimage to Mecca and the celebration at the end of the Hajj. Then there are very public, youth-oriented national celebrations associated with the establishment of the Republic after Turkey prevailed over such imperial powers as France, Britain, Italy and Greece at the end of the First World War.

Ikeda: What are funerals like in Turkey? I assume they involve inhumation.

Yalman: Yes. Cremation is not practised. People have great concern for traditions and respect their elders and ancestry and feel that cremation goes against Islamic traditions. In that

13

sense, Turkish funeral traditions are very similar to those of other Islamic countries.

Ikeda: What about grave sites? Are monuments erected?

Yalman: In some Islamic countries, such as Saudi Arabia, people feel that paying too much attention to graves approaches idolatry. Turks feel this way too. Gravestones are erected, but one must be humble and not attempt to create elaborate tombs. On the other hand, striking monuments have always been erected to the memories of distinguished people such as prime ministers, including Mustafa Kemal Atatürk (1881–1938) himself. These monuments can be controversial in some interpretations.

Ikeda: I see. All gravestones in Soka Gakkai cemeteries throughout Japan are of the same size because we believe that everyone should be equal, both during and after life.

I understand that Muslims must pray five times a day at specific hours. How do ordinary working people perform their prayers?

Yalman: The prayers do not take long: five or ten minutes. It is easy enough to fit them in. Pious people succeed in doing it; there is no difficulty. Prayers can be performed in any clean place.

Ikeda: Are there prayer customs peculiar to Turkey alone?

Yalman: Yes. A very strong, uniquely Turkish tradition follows the teachings of certain Alevi and Bektashi mystics, who say that religious rituals must not be mere ostentation. They must be sincere expressions of appreciation for God and the life given to you. You do not need to pray five times a day. Even once a year may be sufficient, but it must be completely sincere.

Ikeda: Buddhism has certain fixed forms of prayer as religious training but prescribes no specific times for them. The great thirteenth-century Japanese priest and philosopher Nichiren (1222–82) wrote that it is possible to turn life toward happiness by chanting his short formulation of the Lotus Sutra – once a day, once a month, once a year, once a decade or once in a lifetime, as long as it is sincere.[4]

Poor health or the pressure of business may prevent the observance of religious practices. We are urged only to chant it to the best of our abilities. The important thing is the determination to accept the challenge of praying for the sake of self-improvement and to act on the basis of that resolution.

Yalman: The Bektashi/Alevi mystics also teach that fasting throughout the month of Ramadan is unnecessary because conceivably it may be ostentatious. As to the Hajj, Turkish Sufis say it is not necessary to go all the way to Mecca. It is more important to make a pilgrimage into one's own heart. In other words, Turkish humanistic tradition makes Islamic ideas flexible and presents them in a more human way. Some of these mystic traditions may well have originated in Central Asia, where contacts between Islam, Buddhism and Shamanism are known to have existed for centuries. The ancient Silk Road brought many religions into contact with each other, promoting discussion between people from India, China and the West.

Buddhism as peace promoter

Ikeda: The role of religion is not to restrict human beings but to liberate them and turn them towards self-realization. What the twenty-first century needs is religion for the sake of humanity and the ordinary people – not religion for its own sake.

Yalman: Quite right. As is clearly apparent from your important dispute with an authoritarian priesthood, Soka Gakkai stresses humanitarian, not power-oriented, religion.

15

Ikeda: You have always understood us very well, and I am grateful to you. Basically the goal of religion is to make human beings happy by freeing them from suffering. False priests use their religious authority in ways that despise and hamper the people. They overemphasize ceremonies and ritual – especially those connected with funerals – as ways to make money. In other words, they employ religion and religious offerings to rob the people. Soka Gakkai takes the initiative in striving to replace this kind of authoritarianism with a revitalized religion that serves the best interests of the people.

Yalman: When something similar happened in Turkey, attempts were made to break with the formalistic, ritualistic aspects of Islam and to enter the much more sincere interior world of the human being.

Ikeda: Buddhism advocates conformity with local manners and mores and with the climate of the times. Of course, religious fundamentals must not be sacrificed, but Buddhists should always respect the culture of the land they live in and try to contribute as good members of local society.

We are proud that, without becoming either fanatical or ritualistic, we focus on the individual and devote ourselves to universal spiritual satisfaction. In this way, Soka Gakkai International now has a presence in 192 nations and regions. To become truly global, a religion must demonstrate understanding and tolerance of the cultures of other nations.

Yalman: In response to the prejudiced and mistaken opinions sometimes voiced about Soka Gakkai International, I have this to say. From what I have seen, Soka Gakkai and you, Mr Ikeda, are making real contributions to peace. By engaging in direct dialogue with many very intelligent people around the world you establish resonances that go beyond local philosophies and cultures. Your work resonates directly with the teaching of the Buddha. As you will remember, the Buddha tried to make peace among tribes engaged in bloody feuds. Your working method is similar – the pacifist Buddhist tradition of using dialogue to promote union is extremely important.

Ikeda: Your praise is too generous. Stressing dialogue and resisting oppression from power and authority are both the starting point of real tolerance and the permeating spirit of Buddhism.

Yalman: Buddhism seems to have no history of aggressive domination except when hijacked by national or ethnic powers – as we see today, tragically, in parts of south-east Asia and even in Sri Lanka. However, our recent experience in Sri Lanka, Myanmar, Thailand and elsewhere shows that the respected symbols and traditions of Buddhism can be manipulated with great effect by hypocritical politicians and priests. It is true that, before he became a Buddhist, King Ashoka (304–232 BCE) was involved in expansion and invasion. After he became a Buddhist, however, he realized that it was better to be peaceful rather than warlike. This message of peace instead of war is still absolutely vital today. Leaders who claim the honourable mantle of Buddhism must ponder that message, and live up to it.

Ikeda: In King Ashoka's time – as, sadly, in our own – war as a way to solve problems was generally accepted. After he converted to Buddhism, however, the king saw that, far from solving problems, force only creates many new ones. And he courageously drew attention to this. As you suggest, it is absolutely vital for the leaders of our world today to lend a humble ear to Ashoka's teachings.

Yalman: The difference between the activities of an institution dedicated to peace, such as Soka Gakkai, and those of some Christian churches is that, with its evangelizing tradition, Christianity tries to impose a particular interpretation of history and to convert people to it. Some aspects of this are very dangerous. In the Middle East, it makes for considerable misunderstanding and tension among Christians, Jews and

Muslims. This tension is likely to increase – leading not to peace, but war. Consequently, one wonders about the activities of some evangelical churches.

With Soka Gakkai and Buddhist thought, however, this danger does not arise. Buddhism, properly understood, is much more tolerant, does not try to convert and is directly involved in promoting peace. That is why your activities and those of Soka Gakkai are generally welcome in many countries.

Ikeda: Though a Buddhist devotee himself, King Ashoka did not deny other religions. He respected them all. In other words, he clearly endorsed freedom of religion. His well-known pacifist diplomacy entailed dispatching emissaries of peace to various countries and districts such as Greece, Syria, Egypt, Macedonia and Asia Minor. Wherever they went, they consistently acted in a spirit of compassion, transcending differences of language and customs. They constituted what might be called an ancient Peace Party.

The world today is greatly in need of pacifist actions like those of King Ashoka. On the basis of Buddhist humanism, we at Soka Gakkai International strive to emulate his example and are resolved to respect diverse philosophies, cultures and mores, to learn from each other and overcome difference as we work in the areas of peace, culture and education at the level of the ordinary masses.

TWO

Loyalty to All Humanity

Cultivating enduring amity

Ikeda: Soka University of America (SUA), which opened in May 2001, is growing. By 2005, we had students in all four years of the standard undergraduate course. Furthermore, our student body is made up of people from all over the world. As a Turkish student – one of our earliest – said, SUA really teaches diversity.

Yalman: That is wonderful. I feel certain that Soka University of America will grow into one of the finest institutions of learning and teaching in the country. An important country with a complex, diverse population, the United States extends its influence, both for good and ill, to all parts of the world.

Ikeda: One of the goals of this dialogue is to cultivate enduring amity between your country and mine. Achieving that goal requires candour. That is why there is a page in the history of the Turkey–Japan relationship that must be examined.

In the thirteenth century, as the Ottoman Empire was quickly rising to power, Mongols invaded Japan. In the turmoil surrounding this historic event, the shogunate government in Kamakura peremptorily beheaded five Mongol emissaries in a barbaric act – inexcusable on either humane or diplomatic grounds. Grieved at the deaths of these innocent foreigners, Nichiren (whom we of Soka Gakkai revere) fearlessly upbraided the shogunate government. He was inspired to do this because Buddhism is a philosophy that respects life, strives for peace and promotes cultural exchange. One of the executed emissaries was of Turkish descent.

Yalman: I knew there was a person of Turkish descent among the diplomats and that he met a tragic end.

Ikeda: I mentioned this incident in conversations with the Mongolian premier and ambassador to Japan. The former prime minister, Nambaryn Enkhbayar, has said that cultural exchanges are essential to the mutual understanding we must have if we are to go beyond past misfortunes. Indisputably, such exchanges among ordinary people transcend national postures and are the best way to build true friendship.

Yalman: Your words express your profound humanism.

Ikeda: The extent to which Buddhism teaches the dignity of life is expressed in the statement, 'One day of life is more valuable than all the treasures of the major world system.'[1] The vortex of violence and destruction characteristic of our own age has the ironic effect of reinforcing the importance of non-violence and dialogue in the name of the dignity of life. I hope that this dialogue between you and me will be key to a future of amity for Turkey, Japan and the rest of the world.

Dramatic starting point

Yalman: Historically, relations between Turkey and Japan have not been extremely close. Perhaps for this very reason it is important to shed light on the limited exchanges that have taken place. Organizations that research into this topic will be mutually useful in promoting friendship between our two countries.

Ikeda: You are no doubt well aware of the incident that served as the starting point of modern Japan–Turkey friendship. In September 1890, a typhoon sank the Turkish warship *Ertugrul Firkateyni* off the shore of Wakayama Prefecture on her way back to Turkey after concluding a peaceful exchange with Japan. An imperial mission was onboard. Local fishermen did their utmost to rescue survivors. In spite of their efforts, however, nearly 600 lives were lost. Newspapers all over Japan reported the tragedy, and donations poured in to erect a stone cenotaph, where memorial services are conducted to this very day. I understand this dramatic story of friendship has been passed down from generation to generation in Turkey too.

Yalman: Yes, it has. Close relations between Japan and Turkey started in the late nineteenth century with a famous exchange of diplomatic envoys. First, Japanese representatives were dispatched to Turkey in the name of the Meiji emperor. The Ottoman sultan responded by sending his own minister to Japan. He was on the ship sunk by the typhoon off Wakayama Prefecture. To this day, the Turkish people remember the event, which draws them closer to the Japanese. The Turkish navy is still grateful for the noble, courageous Japanese fishermen who saved the lives of Turkish sailors.

Ikeda: Among the many Turks with whom I have exchanged ideas, I regard my talks with the late president Turgut Özal as having been especially important. He presented me with a Turkish medal on the occasion of the centenary of the establishment of relations between Turkey and Japan.

An unforgettable episode illustrates his sense of affinity with Japan. At the outbreak of the Iran–Iraq war, in 1980, about 200 Japanese businessmen found themselves stranded in a hotel in

Tehran. President Özal saved the day for them. When Japan pleaded that the crisis was too dangerous to send a rescue plane, President Özal said that the crisis was precisely why help was so essential. He sent a Turkish plane to Tehran to rescue the Japanese businessmen. I should like to take this opportunity to reiterate the gratitude of the Japanese people.

Yalman: We are honoured to receive it. I am always delighted by deepening exchanges between Japan and Turkey.

Ikeda: Turks say, 'You know who your real friends are when you're down and out.' While we are on the topic of Turkish sayings, I might mention an interesting one to the effect that being treated to a cup of coffee lingers in the memory for forty years. The reason being that, at one time, coffee was a costly drink reserved for special guests. Being treated to it was thus a memorable favour.

Both Turkey and Japan are subject to earthquakes. In 1999, a horrendous quake in Turkey took 17,000 lives – three times as many as those lost in the Hanshin earthquake that hit Japan in 1995. Aid teams were immediately dispatched to Turkey. In the hope of promoting the quickest possible recovery, Soka Gakkai joined other organizations in aid donations. It was our way of making some small recompense for the help the people of Turkey, and especially former president Özal, have extended to us.

Yalman: Actually, we Turks are the ones who should be grateful.

Linguistic similarities

Yalman: In addition to historical exchanges of these kinds, other factors – language, customs and culture – lead some people to think the Japanese and Turkish peoples have the same ethnic roots and are, in a sense, sibling peoples.

As I mentioned before, the Japanese and Turkish languages are thought to be similar. Specialists tell me the grammatical structure of the two is similar. The object of a sentence precedes the verb, and the subject may be omitted, because inflections of the verb imply the subject.

Japanese people learn Turkish fast. I once had a brilliant Japanese assistant who, to my amazement, learned to speak Turkish fluently in four or five months. Similarly, Japanese tourists are always surprised to discover how well ordinary Turkish shopkeepers have picked up Japanese.

Ikeda: Are the languages similar in pronunciation?

Yalman: To my ear, Japanese sounds so much like Turkish that, when in Japan, I feel as if I ought to understand what the local people are saying. In Japanese, *ii-desu* means something is good; in Turkish, we say *ii-dir* – the same *ii* sound signifying good in both languages. There are many other similar instances. Black stone is *kuro-ishi* in Japanese and *kara-tash* in Turkish. God of heaven is *tentei* in Japanese and *tanri* in Turkish. In spite of these similarities in sounds and grammatical structure, however, the etymologies are different because Turkish has borrowed many words from Persian and Arabic, whereas Japanese has borrowed a lot from Chinese and other languages.

Ikeda: I heard that there are some disconcerting cases of phonetic similarities between words of strikingly different meanings.

Yalman: Yes. For instance, a foreigner in Turkish is called *yabanch (yabancı)*, which sounds like Japanese *yabanjin* or barbarian. Turks call a daughter *kuzu (kız),* which in Japanese means trash. When in Japan, I must be careful about using the Turkish word *yabancı.*

Ikeda: In addition to Turkish, you are fluent in German, French, Italian, Singhalese and English. I understand that a

German tutor taught you German as a small child, even before you learned Turkish. Under the Ottoman Empire, Istanbul was a cosmopolitan city where thirty or forty different languages were spoken. To what extent did local Turkish circumstances and history influence you in general, and your interest in language studies in particular?

Yalman: Many ethnic groups coalesce in Turkey. In Istanbul, numerous languages are spoken: this gave me a chance to learn and become increasingly interested in foreign tongues. I have always had a great urge to study Japanese. Perhaps if I had more time I would learn to speak it more fluently.

Ikeda: I admire your great love of learning.

Yalman: Language is a basis of ethnicity. Similarities between the Japanese and Turkish languages suggest deep connections. We share some very interesting customs as well. For instance, the great Japanese fondness for communal bathing is typical of the Turks too. The Japanese sit at a tap and wash themselves before they enter the bath. The Turks do the same thing. In Western Europe, on the other hand, bathing was once considered a dangerous way to spread diseases. Out of fear of getting sick, Queen Elizabeth I of England is said to have taken baths rarely – once a year perhaps, if that often. This fear of bathing influenced the development of perfumery, especially in France, as historians tell us. Ancient customs, such as bathing, go very far back in history and really bring the Japanese and Turks together in a profound way.

Ikeda: How about children's games?

Yalman: Turkish children are just like Japanese children – they play with kites, tops and marbles; they play hopscotch. In this regard, there is no great difference between Japan and Turkey.

Land of many proverbs

Ikeda: Turkey has a wealth of proverbs, two of which I have already alluded to. Folk sayings of this kind mirror national culture vividly. We have already mentioned the cultural similarities between Turkey and Japan. This makes me wonder whether we share similar proverbs. For instance, in Japan we say 'Time reveals the lie' and 'Lying is the start of stealing.' Do you have anything similar in Turkish?

Yalman: We say, 'Lies last only as long as liars' money' and 'A burning candle lives longer than a lie.' The feelings behind these sayings resemble those expressed in the Japanese proverbs you quoted.

Ikeda: Every nation has its liars and enviers of justice.

Another Turkish proverb has to do with the way decadent leaders destroy the organizations they lead: 'Fish rot from the head first.' In other words, rulers of states and organizations are the first to go bad. Josei Toda, my mentor and the second president of Soka Gakkai, used to say that leaders define an organization. All responsibility rests on their shoulders.

In Turkish you say, 'Gold is tried by fire, people by hardship.' Buddhism teaches the same kind of wisdom: 'Put into flames, a rock simply turns to ashes, but gold becomes pure gold.'[2] 'Iron, when heated in the flames and pounded, becomes a fine sword. Worthies and sages are tested by abuse.'[3]

Yalman: The thoughts are really the same. Because of its former vast geographical extent, Turkey came into contact with Central and Southern Asia and with India. Consequently, our culture includes elements that, instead of being distinctly Turkish, either originated from or were influenced by Buddhism.

Ikeda: I am very fond of the Turkish proverb 'Mountains don't get together; people do.' The loftiest mountains are condemned to proud isolation. People, however, can get together. Though puny as individuals, human beings can accomplish much if they combine their powers.

Yalman: In other words, human beings have a great potential for action.

Ikeda: In that sense, the kind of wisdom represented by our dialogue is exclusive to human beings working together.

More than thirty years ago, when Arnold J. Toynbee and I were conducting our dialogue, a summit meeting of world leaders was taking place in England. While commenting on it, Professor Toynbee said that, even though it was the current focus of attention, the summit meeting was only ephemeral, whereas the modest dialogue he and I were engaged in would endure for generations. The same is true of this dialogue with you.

Yalman: I too am certain that this dialogue between a Japanese man and a Turk is an extremely worthwhile undertaking. Across the great Asian continent, it brings the two ends of the ancient Silk Road together.

Fast or slow to act

Ikeda: As this episode about former Turkish president Süleyman Demirel, whom I met in 1992 when he was prime minister, illustrates powerfully, Turks are good at getting things done. At a meeting with the Japanese prime minister, President Demirel (as he was by then) announced his wish to strengthen Turkey–Japan ties by establishing a high school where all instruction would be in Japanese, and he requested support for the project. Because the president had made this announcement without forewarning, the Japanese Ministry of Foreign Affairs received the pronouncement with mistrust. However, immediately after his return to Turkey, Mr Demirel put the plan into action so fast that the Japanese government was compelled to respond quickly.

Yalman: Undeniably, owing to his initiative, Japanese-language schools have increased in number since the president's visit to Japan.

Ikeda: In everything they do, the Japanese prepare thoroughly and strive for perfection but are slow to move into action. Their poor proficiency in second languages reflects these traits. Because they are afraid of making mistakes, they are reluctant to take the initiative in conversation. The Turks, on the other hand, leap into action at once and carry out surveys, preparations and planning simultaneously for the project in hand. Of course, each approach has its advantages and disadvantages. However, in radically changing modern societies, decisiveness, execution and speed are always in demand. Responsiveness helps good organizations develop, whereas poor response spells stagnation. Speed can be said to determine victory – in this regard, Turks' powers of speedy action are a great plus.

Yalman: It is generous of you to say so. I should like to add loyalty to the traits you have already listed as common to both Japanese and Turks. The idea of loyalty is very strong in Japan, as it is in Turkey. Important cultural values – loyalty, discipline and courtesy – influence actions. Popular loyalty enabled Turkey to protect its independence from the nineteenth and into the twentieth century, in the face of imperialist incursions from the great European powers. The same is true of Japan.

Ikeda: An interesting observation. But in Japan, historically, loyalty had the strong negative effect of fomenting rabid militarism.

Resisting imperialism

Yalman: Other countries also escaped domination by the West. For example, in spite of great oppression from the French and British in the nineteenth century, Thailand preserved her independence. Another candidate for inclusion in this group might be Iran, although it was occupied by Russia and Britain in both world wars.

Ikeda: I have fond memories of Iran, which I visited on two occasions – once in 1962 and again in 1964. Professor Majid Tehranian of the University of Hawaii, with whom I have published a dialogue under the title *Global Civilization: A Buddhist–Islamic Dialogue* and who heads our peace studies institute, is a native of Iran.

Yalman: The experiences of one Japanese man who lived in Turkey during an exciting revolutionary period are extremely interesting. As military attaché to the Japanese embassy in Turkey, Kingoro Hashimoto (1890–1957) witnessed the reforms carried out by Mustafa Kemal Atatürk during the 1920s. Upon returning home, Hashimoto promoted a course of national reform centred around the military and argued that Japanese military power should be on a par with that of Western nations. He subsequently attempted a coup d'état, which failed.

Ikeda: This incident reveals the great influence the brilliant Atatürk could exert. Hashimoto's failed coup d'état resulted in a series of terrorist acts and the rise to eminence of the military. Josei Toda kept an watchful eye on yet another coup d'état carried out by a group of young officers on 26 February 1936, and discussed it with me later. These bloody events proved that attempts to solve problems through violence are never permissible under any circumstances.

Yalman: Turkey and Japan both resisted Western imperialist powers. They both have very strong ideas of independence and national identity. This should promote mutual understanding. And, indeed, there have been no disputes between the two countries. Everything is in place for a profound friendship. I see a great future for Japanese–Turkish relations.

Warm feelings toward Japan

Ikeda: You speak of friendly feelings toward the Japanese people. Specifically, what image do the people of Turkey have of Japan?

Yalman: To mention only one of many possible instances of the good impression the Japanese make in Turkey, I might mention Prince Mikasa and his 2002 visit on an archaeological survey. As a token of goodwill he wore a red T-shirt with the star and crescent of the Turkish flag printed on it in white. The people were overjoyed to see him walking around wearing the Turkish flag. Later they felt all the more honoured when they learned that he wore it deliberately because of its resemblance to the Turkish flag, and that he probably would not have honoured the flag of any other country in the same way.

Ikeda: Understanding local feelings and acting in ways that promote friendship are important.

Yalman: As another illustration of creating good relations with the local people, Japanese tourists sometimes get married according to Turkish custom. They travel to small villages where the villagers are delighted to help them celebrate.

Such cordiality and amity express good human relations in ways rarely observed between Turkey and European nations. Clearly the Japanese make a good impression on the Turks.

Ikeda: What instances of Japanese influence on the people of Turkey can you cite?

Yalman: Turkey and Japan have both tried very hard to modernize; Japan has had greater success. The reorganizing of society into a great industrial nation is especially wonderful – through discipline and self-sacrifice, Japan has advanced to a place of pre-eminence in the industrialized world.

We have immeasurable admiration for Japanese success in the field of education too. Promotion of education has eliminated illiteracy, won the battle with illness and hunger, and cultivated reliability in the hearts of the people. In this sense, the Japanese are a model for others, what the Persians call a *merjii-taklid* – a source for emulation.

Ikeda: Thank you for your generous enumeration of Japan's good aspects. What are your expectations of Japan in the years to come?

Yalman: As I have indicated, its development of a distinctive civilization and economy makes Japan a beacon of light for the rest of the world.

People in Istanbul jumped for joy at the news of the Japanese victory over the Russian Empire at the battle of the Tsushima Strait in the Russo-Japanese War of 1904–5. It was the first time a constitutional Asian country had defeated a Western autocracy.

Ikeda: Marshal Heihachirō Tōgō and General Maresuke Nogi became so famous as a result of the war that Turks named their newborn children after them. I understand that some shops in Turkey still bear their names.

Yalman: That is true. Not just Turkey, but other non-Western countries also regard Japan with respect and great interest. In addition to political stability and startling economic growth, in the midst of modernization, Japan has performed the amazing feat of preserving its distinctive traditional culture. This inspires nations such as India, Sri Lanka, Egypt and Turkey to take hopeful pride in their own venerable civilizations.

The Japanese are warmly welcomed far and wide. For instance, the French anthropologist Claude Lévi-Strauss (b.1908) always wanted to talk to Japanese people he encountered in Paris. Sharing that desire, I am one of the people who see Japan as pointing out new directions for the whole world.

The common good

Ikeda: To meet your expectations, the Japanese must make greater contributions to humanity. At a time when Japan was concentrating on becoming what was called a 'prosperous nation through military might', Tsunesaburo Makiguchi prophesied that at some point it would become necessary to afford pre-eminence to humanitarian competition rather than military or economic competition. I am painfully aware that, for us to be respected as humanitarians, we Japanese must think internationally and expand our humane support activities.

What traits do you see as essential qualifications for leadership?

Yalman: This is an important issue. People in both the East and the West are deeply disappointed in world leaders for having allowed – indeed, encouraged – festering troubles to slide into terror, war and chaos. Very few current politicians have a grand vision. Creative people are in demand, as are people with the universal spirit of brotherly love who understand the desire for peace and can direct people towards its attainment. In addition, surely the high moral qualities espoused by many religions are also indispensable in a leader.

Gandhi, who gave up his life in pursuit of peace, used to say that we must cling to truth (*satyagraha*). Ends do not justify means: the nature of the means employed determines the nature of their end result.

Ikeda: I agree. The ethical collapse of Japanese political leaders has long been criticized. Any high-placed person too absorbed in worldly success and economic stability to exert the greatest efforts for the sake of ordinary people is unqualified to be a leader. The source of creativity, action and vision is surely compassion and eager devotion to the common good. Your advice on how we should cope with this essential issue would be appreciated.

Yalman: A nation that has built a unique, homogeneous, enduring civilization tends to become self-absorbed. Some people hope that Japanese society will become more open to the world. It is felt that open external exchanges – not merely in communications and the information industry, but also on the intellectual and cultural planes – are in order. That is why I prize the wonderful faith with which you and Soka Gakkai are trying to open Japan to the world, through vigorous international dialogues and cultural exchanges in many parts of the globe.

Ikeda: Unfortunately, in Japan internationalism is slow to develop. We tend to forget history and try to eradicate the past. After defeat in the Second World War, Japan quickly became rich, then haughty and arrogant. These three traits – ignorance of internationalism, historical forgetfulness and arrogance – are Japanese failings. Unless they are corrected, no nation will want to have anything to do with us. Portents of this are already becoming apparent.

Unless we work for the happiness of peoples everywhere, our prosperity will be meaningless. It is too late to confine loyalty – which you identify as a trait common to the Turks and the Japanese – within national boundaries. Loyalty to all humanity is now absolutely essential. The Soka Gakkai movement aims to cultivate awareness of global citizenship in the minds of the Japanese people by working for the advantage not of a single nation, but of all humankind.

THREE

Peace Within and Without

Atatürk's reforms

Ikeda: To worldwide interest, negotiations for Turkey's entry into the European Union (EU) got underway in October 2005.

Yalman: Yes. Everyone in Turkey was delighted. We all hope that, working together, Turkey and Europe can provide the world with a model of universal humanitarianism and avoidance of conflicts between civilizations.

Ikeda: For Christian and Islamic nations to combine on the basis of shared ideals of democracy and market economy sets an example for coexistence and shared prosperity. Though it is forecast to take more than a decade to achieve, Turkey's entry into the EU will have great significance for human history.

Turkey has cooperated with Europe since the days of its first president Mustafa Kemal Atatürk. My conversations about him with many Turkish thinkers, including the late president Turgut Özal (1927–93), have impressed me with the profound respect in which he is held.

Yalman: Yes. He was really a most astonishing figure – one of the most remarkable people of the twentieth century. Before the Second World War, when practically everyone overlooked the interests of the Third World, alone and unaided he stood up against the aggressive imperialism of great powers such as England and France. Both his military and political talents are highly regarded.

Ikeda: He was born at about the same time as the Chinese writer Lu Xun, the Austrian writer Stefan Zweig, the Spanish painter Pablo Picasso, the English historian Arnold J. Toynbee and Soka Gakkai's first president Tsunesaburo Makiguchi. Having lived through such turbulent times, all these men can teach us much.

After founding the Turkish Republic in 1923, Atatürk became its president and initiated numerous reforms. He did away with the caliphate – which had combined religious rule with the secular rule of the sultan – and promoted women's suffrage and the separation of religion and state. His other political, economic, social and cultural reforms included adoption of the solar calendar and discontinuance of the use of Arabic script in writing the Turkish language. The British high commissioner in Turkey at the time said he had never met a man who understood his goals as clearly, or implemented them as decisively, as Atatürk.

Yalman: He changed the country from an ancient Islamic empire to a Western-looking, energetic, modern republic.

Ikeda: Professor Toynbee evaluated Atatürk's reforms as a kind of historic miracle: 'Under the leadership of first president Mustafa Kemal Atatürk (1881–1938), the country made incredible strides forward. This was the period of the Turkish Revolution . . . the Renaissance, the Reformation, the secularist, scientific revolution . . . the French Revolution, and the Industrial Revolution . . . telescoped into a single lifetime . . .'[1]

Yalman: There is much truth in Professor Toynbee's comment. Yes, there is a great deal of truth in what Toynbee is saying. All these things were concentrated in a single period of ten to twelve years. And it was indeed a miracle because it was done without a great deal of destruction, unlike similar events in Russia or China.

Ikeda: I have spoken of President Atatürk's wisdom and triumphal philosophy to students at Soka University, in a speech at Ankara University, and to young people on numerous other occasions. His guiding philosophy of prizing old friends while making new ones corresponds to the philosophy of Soka Gakkai. He longed to enlighten as many Turks as possible. He based everything on the needs of the people, to whom he imparted great self-confidence.

In a famous speech delivered before the Turkish National Assembly in August 1926, he said, 'Every great movement must find its source in the depths of the people's soul, the original spring of all strengths and greatness. Failing this, all is ruin and dust.'[2]

On the eve of Atatürk's revolution, the Ottoman Empire was indeed the 'Sick Man of Europe'. The great powers were gobbling up not only the Balkan Peninsula and the mid-eastern regions, but also the home region of Anatolia.

Yalman: Yes, the same thing was happening to Turkey as had happened to China.

Ikeda: Some high-placed people inside Turkey were eager to protect themselves by helping the invaders. But Atatürk, the father of his country, awakened the people's pride, telling them to hold their heads high because they were the foundation, the soil and the strength of the nation. In war, education and politics, he was always side by side with the ordinary people, sharing their sorrows and joys, and inspiring all with awareness of and pride in being Turkish. He saved the homeland from crisis by changing the hearts and minds of the people and, in

1919, initiating the building of a new Turkey. Tragically, bloody war with invading powers could not be avoided. What was the driving force behind his reforms?

Yalman: The roots of the Atatürk revolution go back to the nineteenth century and involve thinkers such as Ziya Pasha and Namik Kemal. They were the 'Young Turks', as the French called them, who were in Europe immediately before the Paris Commune of 1871, and who brought revolutionary European ideas back to the Ottoman Empire. The nationalist and advocate of European thought, Ziya Gökalp from Diyarbakir in Kurdistan, also influenced reform in Turkey.

Ikeda: These events were taking place in Turkey at a time when Japan was experiencing what is called the Meiji Restoration, when the feudal age officially ended and the first stirrings of democracy were felt.

Yalman: Atatürk's reforms also have roots in the thoughts of Auguste Comte (1798–1857), whose positivism and secularism were a major intellectual force in the nineteenth century. His theorem of order and progress – the words *ordem e progresso* appear on the modern Brazilian national flag – became the formula for the secret society of reformers called the Ottoman Union, which became the political party 'Union and Progress' that eventually led the empire into the First World War. These ideas of cultural reform took shape gradually. Atatürk made many of them legal, but it took time for them to permeate society.

Ikeda: Because it took time, Turkey suffered oppression for a long while. Nonetheless, Atatürk had unshakable faith in the future of his country. He said with pride that in Turkey there were neither oppressors nor oppressed. Some people submit to oppression; others do not. Turkey, he said, belonged in the latter category. We must always follow the Turkish example, crying out against oppression, fighting back and repelling the enemy. As the Turks say, 'Speak out, and you are persecuted; hold your tongue, and your guts boil over.' The passion for justice that informed this saying illustrates the spirit with which Atatürk dragged Turkey towards reform.

Separation of religion and politics

Ikeda: The separation of religion and politics was one of the most salient of his reforms. From the early sixteenth century to its demise, the Ottoman Empire was a sultan-caliphate in which the sultan exercised both political and religious authority. Atatürk's reforms swiftly separated politics and religion. Do you think the separation of religion and politics will last in Turkey?

Yalman: The combination of state and religion is difficult in an Islamic nation. Sultans always used Islamic scholars to establish their legitimacy. Never in authority themselves, the scholars legitimized the power of sultans. Ottoman sultans were deposed if they were declared illegitimate by the scholars. In Iran, a group of Islamic scholars have taken power and created an Islamic state, but this is the first time such a thing has happened in the history of Islam. Actually the Shi'ite interpretation of Islam considers all powers illegitimate except that of one particular imam (supreme leader and descendant of Muhammad) who will someday reappear but has not done so yet. Therefore, many Iranians consider the state that Ruhollah Khomeini (1902–89) established in 1979 illegitimate and yearn for the separation of religion from the state. Many religious people think the same way.

In Islamic terms, a very strong case can be made for allowing people to experience religion without interference from the state. Therefore, separating political authority and Islam is not a very revolutionary act. In my opinion, the Turkish parliamentary system is a much better example of the functioning of a free and modern Islamic state than Iran or other states that claim to operate on Islamic terms. This is a critical matter that people are beginning to understand.

Ikeda: In 1935, Atatürk authorized the participation of women in politics. To give some idea of how farsighted his reforms were it is necessary only to remember that, in Japan, women's suffrage was decreed during the US occupation at the end of 1945 and made law with the adoption of the Constitution in November 1946. It was his belief that a society that deprives women of opportunities for active participation in public life will inevitably lose vitality. The important role women have played in Soka Gakkai International peace movements illustrates how strongly we sympathize with this aspect of Atatürk's reforms.

Yalman: Today large numbers of women are active in Turkish public life. Their education and social role are an extremely important political issue in Turkish society. The education of women is given the highest priority because well-educated mothers mean better-educated children. In general, this is recognized; however, as I mentioned before, we still have a long way to go because traditional society remains suspicious about whether or not women's education might undermine traditional family values.

Education

Ikeda: Believing that, after independence, building a new country would require widespread education, President Atatürk devoted himself wholeheartedly to this issue and founded many new schools. Indeed, his aspiration was to open a new school every day. At the same time, he encouraged teachers to strive to educate the masses in national citizenship.

Education frees people from prejudice and ignorance. As of 1 January 2005, the United Nations (UN) World Programme for Human Rights Education got under way. Because we believe that respect for human rights forms the foundation for peace,

Soka Gakkai International fully supports this programme. Education is the only way to establish such respect firmly in the popular mind, by bringing people together and transcending differences.

Yalman: I agree completely. Education goes beyond differences of background to reveal the things we all have in common. It guides us out of cliquishness and enables us to think from the standpoint of all humanity.

Ikeda: That is true. Education is the Soka Gakkai International point of origin. Our organization grew out of the Society for Value-Creating Education. Our first two presidents, Tsune-saburo Makiguchi and Josei Toda, were both educators. As the heir to their mission, I too have promoted peace, culture and education based on the teachings of Buddhism.

Yalman: Your promotion of education is very wise because religion must not be categorized by denomination or sect.

The important thing is to go beyond superficial labels such as 'Buddhist' or 'Muslim' to find an underlying philosophy and humanity.

Ikeda: That is precisely what I have been insisting for years.

President Atatürk himself was respected as a teacher among teachers. He went from town to town with blackboard and chalk, instructing the people with a system of his own devising for romanizing the spoken Turkish language. A celebrated story relates how Atatürk congratulated and embraced a farmer who was overjoyed at being taught to write his own name. What influence does romanization of the language have in modern-day Turkey?

Yalman: The question of whether the Latin alphabet is appropriate for Turkish is the same kind of debate the Japanese must have had about whether *kanji* (Chinese) characters are appropriate for the Japanese language. Eventually, after great discussion, the Turks decided to do away with the Arabic script. All of a sudden – overnight – Turkey abandoned a writing system that had been in use for a thousand years. This dramatic change was facilitated by the existing low literacy rate. It is argued that the change greatly increased literacy. Though many people feel nostalgia for the beautiful script and for the immense interest in calligraphy it inspired, I believe the change is probably permanent.

It had the important cultural effect of making it much easier for Turkish intellectuals to read Western languages, thus directing their attention westward. On the other hand, it has cut them off from Iran and other culturally important countries that still use the Arabic script.

Changing scripts evidently has very powerful political implications. In order to isolate them from Turkey and Iran, the Soviet Russians compelled the Turkish-speaking peoples of Central Asia to use Cyrillic letters. Now that these people are beginning to regain their independence, they are experimenting with the Latin alphabet. We shall see how the experiment works out

Ikeda: Turkish is now spoken in numerous places outside Turkey. Immigrants in Bulgaria, Greece, Cyprus and Germany use it. In addition, it is spoken in such post-Soviet republics as Kazakhstan, Kyrgyzstan, Uzbekistan, Turkmenistan and Azerbaijan. Moreover, it has become possible to travel more freely and for the people in those countries to engage in dialogue with each other. Subtly, the use of spoken Turkish is repeating Turkey's historical role of connecting neighbouring nations.

Yalman: It was easier for people to communicate when everyone used the Arabic script. Now that there are many different alphabets in use, it has become much more difficult to follow each other's publications. This difficulty may have important future effects.

Atatürk in the eyes of Islam

Ikeda: During a visit to Ankara in 1992, I paid my respects at the Atatürk Mausoleum. I shall always remember how the vast monument with its marble colonnades rises in the clear Anatolian air on a hill overlooking the city. In the visitors' book I wrote:

> Here sleeps a great leader who foresaw the future of the world.
>   I am certain that the world and the youth of Turkey will engrave in their memories the ideals, actions, and history of his Excellency the president and follow in his footsteps.
>   Leader in the salvation of your great homeland, rest in peace.
>   Rest in peace, enfolded eternally in the radiance of glory.

What is the current evaluation of Atatürk?

Yalman: There is little doubt that Atatürk inspired tremendous hope in people struggling against colonialism. In his lifetime, he was venerated as a great hero. My Indian friends tell me that there are more than 2,000 biographies of Atatürk in Indian languages alone. For a while after his death, too, he was considered an absolutely critical reformer of the Islamic world. What has happened since, however, is an interesting story.

As the Islamic world came under increasing pressure from Britain and America, mostly over oil but also regarding Israel and other matters, attitudes toward the West in many Islamic countries have undergone a steady shift. The large oil producers, such as Libya, Iran and Iraq, have especially found the West very aggressive. Concomitantly, opinions in much of the Islamic world tended to turn against advocates of closer relationships with the West. The more extreme Islamic groups no longer admired Atatürk, once regarded as the great hero who had resisted the colonial powers.

Similarly in Turkey, political parties operating on the Islamic platform have been quick to criticize everything that he did and have even tried to undo some of his reforms. In particular they criticized him for being against the veil and for advocating

41

Western instead of Eastern clothes. But, in my opinion, these objections were mostly superficial and symbolic because, once the Islamists got into power, they had to admit that it was actually Atatürk's actions that had made possible the development of free elections and free political parties.

The situation is paradoxical. Atatürk, who disestablished Islam in Turkey and provided the basis for a free and liberal society, made it possible for an Islamist group to enter the political arena and take power.

In this respect, his legacy needs to be re-evaluated by the Islamic world and his true value to be recognized. As a reformer he not so much destroyed the Ottoman Empire, as pioneered new strategies for a free and open society, in which all kinds of political ideas, including Islamic ideas, could flourish together happily.

Escaping tyranny

Ikeda: As I stated in a speech at Ankara University, President Atatürk's finest characteristic was his excellent sense of balance. For example, while warning that the introduction of foreign capital could lead to outside intervention, he enthusiastically invited outstanding foreign educators to Turkey. Unlike contemporary leaders in power such as Hitler, Mussolini and Stalin – who let obsession with power lead them down the path to destruction – to the end, Atatürk preserved self-control and balance. For example, for the sake of Turkish modernization and democratization, he abolished one-party dictatorship and promoted the formation of opposition parties. Although his efforts did not succeed during his lifetime, for an absolute power – as he was – to create an opposition demanded unprecedented courage. He said that Mussolini and Hitler deceived their people by feeding them terrible racist and nationalist ideas. In his view, only people of outstanding qualities and high morality should be allowed to occupy positions of responsibility.

Yalman: I believe the following course of events explains why Turkey had an Atatürk instead of a Hitler or a Mussolini. In the First World War, Turkey fought on the side of Germany and Austria – the losing side. After the war, Germany had to accept the Treaty of Versailles, against which the rise of Hitler was a kind of reaction.

With Turkey, the victorious powers signed the Treaty of Sèvres, which included the dismantling of the Ottoman Empire. But Turkish nationalists rejected and violently opposed the treaty. In other words, for Turkey, the First World War did not end in 1918 but continued after the German surrender, ultimately to end in a kind of victory in 1924. This fact accounts for the great difference between German and Turkish history.

Ikeda: Heavy war indemnities came as a crushing blow to the German people and were a decisive factor in the rise to power of Hitler and the Nazis. Turkey, on the other hand, continued to fight and finally won. Thus the Turkish people were unconstrained by the outside pressures imposed on the old empire. Though still enduring poverty and suffering, under the leadership of President Atatürk they found hope to move forward to the building of a new country. This major difference between Turkish and German history is highly instructive.

Yalman: Turkey was very fortunate not to be involved in the Second World War because this made it possible, after Atatürk's death, gradually to evolve a multi-party democracy. With this system came many new creative ideas and step-by-step modernization. Turkey escaped the tragic and devastating destruction unleashed by the Russian Revolution and the Chinese Cultural Revolution, or the terrible experiences of Cambodia and Vietnam. It has been protected from them by its sense of identity and discipline and by having avoided the great upheavals of twentieth-century Europe and Asia.

Global partnership

Ikeda: One of Atatürk's speeches contains another highly instructive philosophical lesson. He said that to protect individuals, ethnic groups and nations from selfish exploitation, we must empathize with suffering everywhere as if it were our own. In saying this he was proposing a kind of global partnership that I see as the key to human peace and harmony in the twenty-first century. Do you agree?

Yalman: Entirely. Creating such a partnership requires that we all be mutually connected by humanism. The sense of universal humanism has been expressed through the ages by great thinkers and writers and was beautifully re-expressed by my dear teacher Claude Lévi-Strauss, who wrote that we must allow for and respect diversity in such a fashion as to prevent the ideas and activities of one from interfering with the ideas and activities of others. Such humanism is a sense of respect for human beings, a respect for differences; it is acceptance without aggression. Respect must allow diversities to exist, and the diversities must not interfere with each other. This modern sense of humanism attempts to allow individuals and communities to develop in a liberal, open, mutually non-constraining way.

Jean-Jacques Rousseau aptly expresses another important idea when he says that empathy for others is at the root of anthropology. Others must have their own space in which to exist. Empathy and gentle kindness towards other people must be at the root of the new humanism, which will allow Buddhists to be Buddhists, Hindus to be Hindus, Jews to be Jews, Muslims to be Muslims, Christians to be whatever kind of Christian they want to be, Daoists to be Daoists, and Confucians to be Confucians without getting in each other's way.

Ikeda: Persevering, constructive dialogue is essential if we are to prevent cultural differences from becoming hotbeds of aggression and exclusivism. The Toda Institute for Global Peace and Policy Research and the Boston Research Center for the 21st Century provide forums where people of diverse cultural and religious backgrounds can come together for debate and dialogue, leading to mutual understanding.

Yalman: That is a very important undertaking. In the years to come, the peoples of the world must overcome differences in thought, culture and customs; open their minds wide and expand the network of humanism that is the shared wisdom of the human race.

That indeed will be a modern renaissance. Throughout history, the philosophies and cultures of the world have evolved their own fundamental humanisms. In the modern renaissance, these humanisms should become a global symbiosis in which all coexist in mutual respect. In your efforts to expand human togetherness through cross-cultural exchanges of ideas with people from all over the globe, you have become a valuable model of the modern renaissance.

Ikeda: In 1937, the year before he died, President Atatürk said that humanity required a new standard for the sake of solving international conflicts and realizing peace. He went on to say that only actions and interests that served to bring people together, encouraged them to love each other and satisfied their material and spiritual needs could make human beings truly happy. As he perceptively observed, the only way to bring the world happiness and peace is to swell the ranks of people championing this noble idea.

In his day, Turkey was subjected to great pressure due to its relations with contiguous nations, especially with the Great Powers.

Yalman: Yes, but he consistently sought peace and expressed his conviction in the motto 'Peace within the homeland, and peace in the world.'

Ikeda: His consistent quest for peace imbues his refined philosophy with fresh, glowing wisdom from which the world can learn much.

FOUR

Mutual Understanding for a Better World

Ambassador of peace

Ikeda: Through organizations such as the Min-On Concert Association we energetically strive to develop cultural exchanges between Turkey and Japan. One of the most unforgettable people I have encountered in connection with this work is the late, nationally famous singer, Barış Manço, whom I met on several occasions in both Tokyo and Istanbul. He was a treasured friend and a great Euro-Asian artist.

Yalman: He was a celebrated musician. Everybody in Turkey knew him, and he was loved throughout the world.

Ikeda: I first met him at a concert, the Japan–Turkey Goodwill Festival, held in 1991 at the Soka University Auditorium. Harmonizing traditional and new elements, as well as Eastern and Western, he brought 5,000 people to their feet with highly energetic performances of distinctive pop hits. Then, as the crowd went wild, he rushed down from the stage, came straight over to me, and with his arm around my shoulder, said, 'Let's give our very best in the name of peace!'

Yalman: A very dramatic scene! I can imagine how seeing a Turk and a Japanese person united for peace must have excited the audience.

Ikeda: As a cultural ambassador, Mr Manço travelled around the globe on more than a dozen occasions, telling the whole world about one Turk's love of peace. He proudly told me that everything he sings is a product of the culture of the great Ottoman Empire, which flourished for six centuries and stretched across Europe and Asia. He added that he and his contemporaries are the heirs of Turkish tradition – fidelity, strong family ties and respect for others. He especially endeared himself by enumerating these characteristics, which are shared by the Japanese and the Chinese.

Yalman: I agree completely with what Mr Manço said to you. As we have commented before, in private life, Turks and Japanese both stress the importance of harmony with their surroundings.

Ikeda: In the late 1950s, a Turkish song called 'Üsküdara' was very popular in Japan.

Yalman: Üsküdar is the name of a district in Istanbul. Üsküdara means 'to Üsküdar', as in 'on the way to Üsküdar'.

Ikeda: The somewhat rearranged Turkish music of the song captured the hearts of Japanese of both sexes and all ages, probably because it stimulated fond longings for Turkey and its, to us, exotic culture. I believe it produced resonances at a deep spiritual level. I understand that some Turkish folk music is like the kind of Japanese folk songs called *oiwake-bushi*. Both apparently have leisurely, conversational, melodic styles evocative of the emphasis the people of both countries put on harmony between the individual and the surroundings, of which you have just spoken.

Yalman: Some years ago Laurence Pickens, a much-respected friend of mine and a member of both the oriental languages (Chinese) and music departments of Cambridge University, argued that there is a strong historical connection, by way of ancient Central Asia, between the music of Turkey and the *Gagaku* music of Japan. It is an idea that needs to be looked into further.

Music as a cultural bridge

Ikeda: In recent years the Japanese, especially young people, have had chances to appreciate performances by Turkish Whirling Dervishes, who seek elevated spirituality through the whirling dance called *sema*.

In March 1992, Min-On invited members of the Egyptian Arts Group to perform their wonderful Al-Tannoura whirling dances in Japan. I believe the Egyptian version evolved from Turkish religious dances.

Yalman: Yes, the whirling dances were originated by the great Sufi philosopher and poet Rumi.

Ikeda: Rumi was active in Konya, the Seljuk Turkish capital, during the thirteenth century, when Nichiren was active in Japan. His disciples and successors created a profoundly spiritual culture of flourishing poetry, music and dance that spread from Turkey throughout the Islamic world.

A line in one of Rumi's poems goes: 'Listen to the Reed, How it tells its tale . . .' The image of a lone flute player is used as a metaphor for mortal humanity seeking the immortal origins of things.

By the way, the reed flutes used to accompany the dervishes resemble a Japanese instrument called *shakuhachi*.

Yalman: Yes, they are called *ney*. What are the origins of the *shakuhachi*?

Ikeda: It originated in Central Asia and was exported eastwards together with Buddhism; its sound is said to represent the teachings of Buddhism. In a similar way, the sound of the *ney* is likened to the voice of the wise seeker of truth and the faithful seeker of the Way of Islam.

Though as isolated as a reed, the human being can establish verbal contacts with his fellows, the world around him, and things that transcend him. This fundamental aspect of the human being is what Rumi proclaims in the poem I just quoted. His reference to a reed calls to mind the famous statement by Blaise Pascal (1623–62): 'Man is but a reed, the weakest in nature, but he is a thinking reed.'

Yalman: You raise the issue of relationships and communication between countries separated by great geographical distances, such as Turkey and Japan. In doing this you point out the possibilities of rich encounters between different cultures.

Ikeda: My activities are inspired by a desire to be a global citizen enhancing the possibilities of dialogues transcending race, religion and customs. I believe that our shared humanity enables us to understand each other and our responsibility for the future of the Earth.

Yalman: I am honoured to be able to participate in your efforts to that end.

Understanding others

Ikeda: Your field of specialization is cultural anthropology. How do you define it?

Yalman: Definitions vary. In my opinion, cultural anthropology is the attempt to understand other people.

Ikeda: An excellent definition. When did the study of cultural anthropology originate? Which environment did it develop in?

Yalman: In the general philosophical sense of trying to understand other people, cultural anthropology goes back to Ancient Greek thinkers such as Herodotus and Thucydides.

Ikeda: Herodotus' *The Histories* and Thucydides' *History of the Peloponnesian War* remain valuable sources of information about ancient cultures in general, especially those of Egypt and the Orient.

Yalman: To come closer to modern times, there appeared other great people such as Abū Rayhān al-Bīrūnī (973–1048), who wrote about India in his *Kitab al-Hind*, one of the best accounts we have of what was going on in the minds of Hindus of that time. Though himself a Muslim, he wrote fairly and honestly about Indian society.

The attitudes of the French Enlightenment – people such as Voltaire (1694–1778), Rousseau (1712–78) and Diderot (1767–1837) – showed a great deal of interest in other peoples and other ways of thinking.

Ikeda: These were some of the thinkers who helped create modern Europe. Too often modern European beliefs are thought of in Western-centred terms as distinct from, and superior to, the beliefs of the East. Of course, this is not the case. Some of the origins of Eastern thought go back to representatives of the great Islamic tradition, such as Avicenna (980–1037), Averroes (1126–98) and many others, whose ideas reached medieval Europe from Andalusian Spain.

Yalman: An acute observation. Cultural anthropology fits in with the great liberal traditions of universal thought and must include major contributors from the Germanic cultures, such as Goethe or Hegel, and from Russia – Tolstoy, Gogol, Pushkin, Dostoyevsky and others. In their philosophies, we can perceive the implied criticism of colonial and imperial rule by Western countries that informs the intellectual traditions of cultural anthropology.

Above all, Gandhi was deeply influenced by his Muslim friends and by Tolstoy. Once, when he was in London negotiating for Indian freedom, he was asked what he thought of Western civilization. He replied, ironically, 'Western civilization would be a good idea.'

Ikeda: On another occasion he told some Europeans, 'In spite of your belief in the greatness of Western civilization . . . leave some little room for doubt . . .'[1]

Yalman: Cultural anthropology has not always been as noble as my description makes it sound. In the nineteenth century, it was essentially a tool of colonial and imperial powers, who employed the attempt to understand other people in order to control them.

Ikeda: In his book *Orientalism*, the Palestinian-American literary critic Edward W. Said (1935–2003) made the same point. From the eighteenth century until the wave of liberation that took place after the end of the Second World War, many parts of Asia, Africa and Central and South America suffered under the yoke of colonialism. During that period, according to Professor Said, 60,000 books on the Middle East were published in Europe. Certainly some of them reported the inhumanities of colonial rule. Most of them, however, attempted to justify European colonialism and described the colonized regions as culturally inferior and in need of governance and guidance. 'Orientalism' is what he called the colonial rulers' mindset as demonstrated in this vast number of books and reports.

In his view, Orientalism meant all attempts to describe colonies from the standpoint of colonial bureaucracy. He sharply criticized it as a Western device for controlling, remaking and browbeating the Orient.

Yalman: That must be admitted. At the same time we must note that individual scholars varied greatly on this issue. The humanist traditions were always very strong in cultural anthropology. The great nineteenth-century anthropologists in France, Britain and America were extremely sympathetic to the people they studied and made great contributions to the maintenance of their cultures. Many of them strongly opposed the policies of colonial or imperial regimes.

Ikeda: That's right. They worked together in the field and related to the people – not as colonial masters, but as human beings dealing with other human beings.

The following instructive story from a collection of Buddhist stories dealing with the six kinds of bodhisattva practices illustrates two approaches to cultures other than one's own. Long ago in India, a pair of brothers made a commercial trip to another country that was despised as culturally retarded. The younger brother decided that they should first try to understand the minds of the people. The two of them should dress like the locals, speak their language and live as they did. The haughty older brother, however, was unwilling to wear the coarse clothes of the people and insisted on dressing splendidly in the fashion of his homeland.

The younger brother immediately put his own plan into practice. He took part in monthly dance gatherings and enjoyed dancing in a circle to rhythmical music. By blending with their way of life, he won the people's confidence.

But the older brother utilized a magnificent vehicle, which the local people ridiculed, sending him scurrying back to his own land. When the younger brother tried to accompany him, the people lined the road, begging him to stay with them but showering his brother with abuse.

Globalization and cultural anthropology

Ikeda: What motivated you to become a cultural anthropologist?

Yalman: I wanted to understand essentially what makes people and societies work in the twentieth and twenty-first centuries. What mechanism drove the Meiji Restoration in Japan, Atatürk's revolution in Turkey, the Russian Revolution and the Cultural Revolution in China? I wanted to understand the dynamics that induce people to undergo change in the deepest and most profound aspects of their identities as by-products of political movements.

Ikeda: What are the latest cultural-anthropological ideas about what makes people in the twenty-first century work?

Yalman: As understanding other people has become a widespread anthropological concern, we are learning the nature of cultures and how they communicate with each other better. Thanks to accelerating means of communication, such as the mass media, in both good and bad senses, this aspect of globalization has become the most powerful force in the world and will have very profound effects on the future.

Ikeda: The important thing is discovering how to direct cultural communications away from standardization and toward greater enrichment.

Yalman: That is true. Anthropologists are cooperating and demonstrating great interest in how cultures maintain themselves while communicating with other cultures. In this respect, problems related to immigration, emigration, refugees and human rights have become central anthropological concerns everywhere.

Ikeda: They are also matters of immense concern to humanity in general.

Yalman: Instead of studying small cultures as isolated jewels, we now concern ourselves with a much broader investigation of how cultures affect each other and how the increasing influence of world culture through globalization and the powerful use of mass media are having effects everywhere.

However, the colonial impetus to dominate other peoples has not died down yet. We are still witnesses to disastrous policies that have led to atrocious violence, particularly in the Middle East. If the latest report in the reliable British medical journal *Lancet* is to be believed, the total number of people killed in Iraq since the war began is said to be in the order of 650,000 with a margin of error of 200,000! The world may be getting more connected, but it is not getting more peaceful.

Barbarians are people who believe barbarism exists

Ikeda: For a long time people in the West considered themselves sophisticated and all other cultures barbarian. As you have indicated, the first achievement of cultural anthropology was to smash these prejudices and preconceptions.

Yalman: It is absolutely true that cultural anthropology has had a tremendous influence in breaking down the simplistic conception of Western superiority. In this connection we must give due recognition to the role played by the French anthropologist Claude Lévi-Strauss.

Ikeda: He said that barbarians are people who believe that barbarism exists.[2]

Yalman: Yes, the words you quote are very apt. Through his detailed work on the mentalities of so-called simple peoples, Lévi-Strauss showed how, in fact, their mental activities are not all that different, thus eliminating the idea of the 'primitive'.

Lévi-Strauss exploded the idea that there are fundamental differences in mentalities among different peoples. He argued that the mental abilities of human beings everywhere differ little. The only thing that differs is the nature of the problems they think about. There is no fundamental difference between developed, industrial peoples and apparently 'simpler' peoples like the Australian aborigines.

Ikeda: He and other anthropologists teach that, if we want to understand individual people's significance and the profound dignity of humanity as a whole, we must examine customs, cultural societies and communities within their own frames of reference.

Yalman: Yes. In that respect, I think his contribution to a sense of dignity for all peoples everywhere cannot be overestimated.

Intellectual giant

Ikeda: Like Sigmund Freud (1856–1939) and the Swiss linguist Ferdinand de Saussure (1857–1913), Lévi-Strauss has exerted an immense influence on modern society.

Yalman: Yes. I respect him tremendously. The great imagination, precision, and care he demonstrated in dealing with the structure of human thought are extremely valuable. He is the one person who succeeded both in demonstrating similarities between the use of the imagination and symbolism, all the way from the art of primitive peoples to modern art – indicating how these aspects of artistic and imaginative structure and pattern are related. His success in this area makes his probably the most important critical and analytical work in the field of human thought since Sigmund Freud.

Ikeda: Lévi-Strauss subtly analysed the close relationship between society and a people's thought structures. For example, societies that make elaborate distinctions between different kinds of fish might lack words for similar distinctions regarding horses or cows. Members of a fish-oriented society are not retarded because they cannot tell a Jersey from a Holstein.

Yalman: Yes. Lévi-Strauss showed that the thought processes involved in mythology, rituals and religious symbolism, analyzed from a great variety of peoples around the world, differ in no way from the remarkable imaginative and scientific processes that go into the construction of contemporary astronomy.

It is true that our scientific knowledge is based on systematic analysis and experimentation, but essentially the creative thought involved is similar to what is at work in the myths and ideas of simple peoples.

Ikeda: Few of us understand the workings of the electrical appliances we use every day. In that respect we are not very different from people who have never used such appliances. A city-dweller set down in a desert knows at once that he lacks the knowledge to survive in such an environment. It is foolish even to ask who is more culturally adept, the dweller of the desert or the inhabitant of a city full of electrical appliances.

Yalman: Essentially, the difference in ways of thinking is a superficial matter of techniques and memory control. According to Lévi-Strauss, scientific creativity and the structuring of images and symbols differ little from the imagination employed in the thought of unscientific peoples. This important point indicates profound emotional involvement in imagination.

Ikeda: Pride in scientific progress blinds people today to their own natures. In the area of emotions and imagination, it is impossible to call one society more advanced than another.

Yalman: That is very true. For instance, on the basis of what they learn from sophisticated scientific instruments such as the Hubble telescope, astronomers tell us about black holes and millions of galaxies unimaginable distances away.

Ikeda: All of which we are incapable of directly experiencing.

Yalman: Yes, we have difficulty grasping and understanding emotionally the things scientists tell us. Mythology, in the form of media experiences like the *Star Wars* films, engages us and puts scientific theorizing on a human scale where we can begin to comprehend what scientists are telling us.

Ikeda: In a way, such mythology makes scientific knowledge seem more real.

Did you ever meet Claude Lévi-Strauss?

Yalman: Yes. More than twenty years ago, my colleague David Maybury-Lewis and I invited him to Harvard to receive an honorary degree. It was a great pleasure to meet him and share a scintillating conversation about the eccentric aspects of cultural life in the United States and about the customs of people living in the tropics.

Ikeda: Did you have associations with him before that as well?

Yalman: Yes, I had met him about thirty years ago, when he was first appointed to the Académie Française and I had just written a review of his book *The Savage Mind* for the *American Anthropologist*.

Ikeda: In his monumental book, Lévi-Strauss shows definitively that cultures once despised as barbarian actually possess concrete sciences mythologically expressed in highly symbolic ways.

Yalman: That is true. The brilliant analysis in the last chapter of *The Savage Mind* reflects the keen precision of his thought. Recently, a whole edition of the French journal *Le Nouvel Observateur* was dedicated to the work of Lévi-Strauss and was entitled *La Pensée Sauvage*. In his nineties at the time – one of our wise elders – he is a very remarkable person who has had a profound effect upon the thinking of the twentieth and twenty-first centuries.

FIVE

Intercultural Communion

Dialogue as the solution

Yalman: I understand that you have already participated in over 1,600 dialogues. Your method of conducting them is exemplary: first, respect the other party and, second, listen attentively. This is the way to promote understanding among people with different cultural backgrounds. I hope you will long continue in this good work.

Ikeda: Thank you. As a leading cultural anthropologist you have consistently emphasized the importance of dialogue between and among civilizations as the best way to resolve the prejudices and misunderstandings that cause antagonism.

Yalman: It is difficult for anthropologists to speak about the rise and fall of cultures because they keep their noses very close to the present. They are often so involved in the cultures around them that the larger cycles of formation, flourishing and decline seem obscure from the standpoint of cultural anthropology. These cycles are, however, more evident to archaeologists and historical anthropologists.

Ikeda: Cultural anthropology points up the characteristics and strong points of individual civilizations. At the same time, however, it projects a fuller image of human history by relating connections among cultures all over the world. The breath of humanity is detectable in the cultures around us. They are the reality of human society – with its joys, angers, pathos and pleasure. Being involved in them brings one closer to the truth of history.

Yalman: The question of rise and decline has been an issue in the West for a long time, beginning with Spengler's *The Decline of the West* and Toynbee's ideas about the rise and fall of civilizations in terms of challenge and response.

The peril of stereotypes

Ikeda: In the dialogue he and I conducted, Professor Toynbee referred to civilizations and history with candour and modesty. He did not narrowly limit his interest to heroes and rulers. His all-encompassing view of civilization demonstrated profound confidence in the strengths and potential of ordinary humanity.

Yalman: One of our big problems is defining the nature of cultures and civilizations. This is no simple matter. Bernard Lewis, a controversial but gifted observer of the Middle East, has written that, when cultures and civilizations clash, one prevails and the other is destroyed. Therefore, in his opinion, to speak of the cohabitation of cultures and civilizations is mistaken because when they cohabit, the worst aspects of both emerge, and this causes collisions. A few years ago, an important article in the *Wall Street Journal* claimed that Lewis' ideas are behind the pugnacious stance of the United States – especially the American military – vis-à-vis the Islamic world. It was also claimed that Lewis' book was bedside reading for the American president.

Ikeda: In recent years, Bernard Lewis' ideas have been appearing in the Japanese press and academic world, too. I am apprehensive about his notion that cohabitation of cultures causes conflict. It seems to me that his own way of defining a culture can become a cause for conflict.

Yalman: The way Bernard Lewis conceptualizes and essentializes Islam is very dubious. His definition of Islam does not accord with modern Islamic practices – the discrepancy leads him to formulate the idea of high and low Islam.

Ikeda: Lewis' theory has come in for criticism from many quarters, including the philosopher Edward Said.

Yalman: This idea of high and low Islam causes major problems. He is right in saying that an internal debate is taking place among Muslims about accommodation to the realities of the modern world. In this regard, unceasing attacks – military and otherwise – from the West have greatly intensified the terms of discussion. Algeria, Egypt and Iran are good cases in point; but there are others as well.

Indeed much of the so-called 'fundamentalist' activity in the Muslim world is a delayed reaction to destructive, indeed warlike, activities of the major Western powers. The British and the French had long been deeply implicated. They have now been joined by a naïve USA that had no idea of what it was getting into. The result of the arrogance of military power and the ignorance of local cultures is a much increased atmosphere of fear, danger and xenophobia everywhere. It is greatly to be regretted that the conditions that lend themselves to 'asymmetrical warfare' are now the order of the day in many places. It is vital for people who value human life and peace to question the policies that have led us to this dangerous brink.

Ikeda: Stereotypical characterizations of culture – for instance, as somehow behind the times – are easy to understand and popularize but, in their very simplification, they sacrifice richness and diversity. What is more, they may wipe out the possibilities for change in human beings.

Yalman: These are matters of definition. Actuality does not always conform to established definitions. From the viewpoint of actual living people, matters are complex. Living civilizations are rich and elaborate ways of life that human beings can alter.

Ikeda: That is why I say that simplified stereotypes are cause for apprehension.

Yalman: Yes, they are. Like language, culture or civilization is a living thing that changes slowly. Although, once again, we are dealing with definitions, it is difficult to say that a culture or civilization has necessarily declined.

Ikeda: I agree. Change is proof of life.

Yalman: A language that has been defined in a certain way can be said to have died out when it departs from that definition. On the other hand, the point could be made that, instead of dying, it has merely shifted into a different form.

Ikeda: Interpretation makes all the difference.

Yalman: Questions of civilizational rise and decline are largely influenced by prejudice and depend on the observer's viewpoint. It is not always easy to indicate moments of high achievement or tragic destruction.

Ikeda: I see. The same civilization looks different depending on the angle from which it is viewed.

Yalman: Some have claimed that Islam has been declining since the twelfth century, in order to deny the vitality of the Ottoman, Safavid, Mogul and other Muslim societies. Others would say that, on the contrary, Islam is more alive now than ever. It is one of the fastest growing faith communities in the world today. I could claim the same for Buddhism in its many forms, as well as for Hinduism in all its myriad forms of worship. People are turning to these ways of life for a sense of security more eagerly than they did in the past.

Ikeda: Humanity now faces various crises. We therefore need firm spiritual solidarity, which provides people with a sense of security as well as hope and courage.

Yalman: One thing, however, can be said: throughout history, cultures and civilizations have attacked each other. We have learned that they can be destroyed through conquest, slavery and all sorts of other means.

Ikeda: That is a fact of history. Collisions between and among cultures and civilizations would seem to be our destiny. But they must not be allowed to go on forever.

The challenge of globalization

Yalman: Possibly we are witnessing major changes taking place before our eyes.

World cultures are being absorbed into a larger, global, media empire. For this reason groups of people who want to preserve their cultural identities are putting up systematic resistance to globalization and homogenization.

Ikeda: As the considerable amount of discussion afforded the topic of revivalism indicates, Japan, too, is witnessing a similar trend.

Yalman: It appears that we are beginning to see the challenges that Toynbee quite rightly pointed out. The cultures of the world are being challenged.

Ikeda: How we respond to these challenges is a matter of utmost importance.

Yalman: Some respond by closing in on themselves – becoming dogmatic, growing more enclosed and trying consistently to maintain their true identities in the face of great challenges from the world media.

Ikeda: Tragically but undeniably, for about a decade, as nationalism has intensified, friction and opposition have replaced earlier contacts and exchanges. Inter-civilization clashes are widely discussed. With your own cultural-anthropological wisdom, how do you think we should re-evaluate intercultural relations?

Yalman: One absolutely critical evaluation of dominance and destruction between civilizations comes from the work of my colleague here at Harvard, Samuel P. Huntington.

Ikeda: Yes, his work has stimulated extensive discussion in Japan, as elsewhere.

Yalman: In his *The Clash of Civilizations*, Huntington deals in particular with the relationship between the West and Islam, in a way similar to the approach of Bernard Lewis. He argues that, in a sense, the United States needs an enemy to maintain a sense of its own cultural unity. Lamentably, the relationship between Islam and the West revolves around stereotypes on both the Islamic and Western sides. This has led to an exaggerated sense of 'Islamophobia', both in Europe and in the USA.

Ikeda: Such stereotyping generates a cycle of mutual misunderstanding and animosity. Western society now talks in patterns and clichés removed from the actuality of Islam, while the Muslim world speaks of Western culture as materialism devoid of spiritual tradition. In this way, both aggravate misunderstanding and animosity.

Ignorance breeding prejudice

Yalman: There is, however, a big difference between the way Westerners conceptualize Islam and the way Muslims conceptualize the West.

The Muslims' problem with the West has to do with imperial and colonial policies in Islamic countries. These are matters not of civilization, but of political and military control. The number of military actions, including covert CIA operations, carried out in the Middle East is beyond counting. Since the nineteenth century, Western powers such as France and Britain, and more recently the United States, have been constantly involved in the political life and future of these countries, and have manipulated them as much as they could. So it is not surprising that Muslims feel challenged by Western power and demonize Westerners for what they did, especially in the nineteenth and twentieth centuries. Evidently the twenty-first century is no exception.

The Western attitude towards Islam is one of lack of comprehension. In the West, ignorance about the impressive achievements of Islamic civilization results in caricatures used to generate a sense of grievance and crisis against Islamic countries.

Ikeda: Professor Majid Tehranian and I agree that failure to recognize the Muslim origins of many of the scientific technologies, which developed rapidly in the West after the Renaissance, results in a most inadequate understanding of Islam.

Yalman: Western misunderstanding, however, in no way justifies terrorism. The events of 9/11 were indeed extremely destructive on both sides and served only to further the agenda of people who would like to see a greater division between the West, Islam and other civilizations.

Ikeda: Terrorism is an absolute evil that resolves nothing.

Yalman: Although he has certainly drawn attention to some serious problems in the way people perceive each other, to my mind, Samuel Huntington has insufficiently emphasized the role of symbolism and scapegoating. Stereotypical conceptions of 'the other' as enemy can be extremely destructive to both parties.

Ikeda: I agree entirely. They breed opposition and division.

Yalman: Instead, your ideas of empathy and person-to-person exchanges contrast sharply with the dangerous and negative outcomes of demonizing.

Tools of nationalism

Ikeda: The time has come for us all to re-examine history honestly, without prejudice and preconceptions. For instance, we should pay more attention to cases in which exchanges between Islam and the West have been highly productive. A case in point is Ibn Rushd – Averroes as he is known in Europe – who was born in Cordoba, Spain. His name has gone down in history as a great Aristotelian scholar whose philosophy exerted a great influence on Christian theology in Europe.

Yalman: The life of Ibn Rushd has much to teach us regarding how Islam and Europe can coexist peacefully. Incidentally, the Roman philosopher Seneca was also born in Cordoba.

Ikeda: At one time, harmony in Cordoba was so prevalent that a single mosque accommodated Muslim worship on Fridays and Christian worship on Sundays. After the creation of a centralized Spain as a result of the unification of Castile and Aragon in the fifteenth century, however, Jews and Muslims alike were persecuted and expelled.

Yalman: That is true. It is worth noting that Jews who were driven out of Spain were invited to live in the Ottoman Empire, where cordial relations were maintained among the Christian, Islamic and Jewish elements of the population. Though many nineteenth-century Western philosophers adopted negative approaches to the issue, numerous surviving records show that the empire permitted and supported various activities on the part of Christians and Jews, many of whom held high official positions, almost to the end of the First World War in 1918.

Ikeda: In the past, even in the former Yugoslavia, famous for religious antagonism, Muslims and Christians got along well. On one occasion, Muslims presented Catholics with a chapel. As this and other aspects of history reveal, the problem is not direct hostility between religions but narrow-minded nationalism and its use of religion and race as tools for inciting conflict. In daily life, peaceful coexistence among religions is completely possible. Indeed, numerous major cities around the world provide real examples of how religions coexist harmoniously and contribute to prosperity. However, when national authorities and the mass media generate stereotypical images that distort this true state of affairs, conflict and confusion arise.

Yalman: I agree. In the increasing conflict of the present, the role of anthropology is to present the real situation as it is and to show the many ways in which the two sides can understand each other.

Ikeda: Although it is not cultural anthropology, Edward Said's *Out of Place: A Memoir* is thought-provoking because of the detailed picture it gives of the author's childhood and adolescence in Palestine – set out as a film director might do, if he wanted to leave a record of everything he had experienced. Like children everywhere, the youthful Said loves playing soccer and hates piano lessons. He respects adults who help the unfortunate and is enraged by social injustice. The image is of a child – neither refugee nor terrorist – living out his life against the background of Palestine's tragedy. While sometimes on the verge of being defeated by the worries and angst of youth, he refines his sense of social wrong. Far from being standardized and bland, the boy has a strong personality and a compulsion to expand his feelings of sympathy.

As you say, the global media empire tries to present fictional, standardized images divorced from reality. To avoid being deceived by such contrivances, we must see people as they are, as Edward Said paints the boy. Free of prejudice, we must recognize our common humanity.

I always remember how my own mentor, Josei Toda, used to say that the problems confronting humanity would be quickly resolved if Shakyamuni, Nichiren, Muhammad, Jesus Christ and Confucius could get together for an exchange of opinions. Though each would certainly have his own ideas and articles of faith, all would perceive and empathize with human suffering and agree in wanting to alleviate it.

Yalman: Yes. Such a conference might not guarantee total agreement but would certainly be a major first step.

Empathy with the suffering of all

Ikeda: The most important thing in dealing with global problems now is empathy for every single suffering human being.

Frequent reports of tragic religious conflict cause some people to adopt the easy, simplistic notion that different religions cannot coexist peacefully. But ordinary human lives tell a different tale – the story of how people of diverse religious backgrounds do live together as parents, children, brothers, sisters and friends.

Yalman: Very true. Our experience as Turks proves how people who seem most heterogeneous can maintain highly amicable relations. Building relationships that take the other

70

parties' humanity into consideration is an enriching experience free of fear.

Ikeda: Today we need a view of history focused on individual human beings and individual lives and their daily activities. Adopting this approach sheds clear light on the history of Islamic–Christian exchanges. Now is the time for us to evaluate not only history, but also science, technology and politics on the basis of their contributions to individual human happiness.

Yalman: I am in total agreement. As long as they use their political elements with caution and a sense of respect, there is no reason for cultures and civilizations not to enrich each other.

There is much that the West can teach Islam, but similarly there is much that Islam can teach the West. In terms of human relations, equality and social justice, there are immensely rich areas in the Islamic tradition that the West would find it worthwhile to cultivate. Alternatively, there is much that Muslims need to think about concerning universal education and the role played by women in a free society.

Ikeda: Certainly the Islamic tradition of social responsibility towards the poor and unfortunate and towards women and children can help correct Western civilization's excessive concentration on economic interests. Civilizations that unassumingly incorporate the superior viewpoints of other civilizations as the valuable spiritual heritage of all humanity are the ones that will achieve true prosperity in the future.

Yalman: That is precisely what I would say. I have the greatest respect for your fair assessment of Islam.

Ikeda: In 2005, in order to cultivate mutual understanding among different faiths and traditions, the United Nations launched its Alliance of Civilizations initiative. The project was proposed by Turkey and Spain. I expect great things from such international movements aimed at avoiding clashes and bringing different civilizations together through dialogue and understanding.

SIX

Empathy and Our Shared Humanity

_____

The attempt to understand

Ikeda: Your definition of cultural anthropology as an 'attempt to understand other people' is lucid and universally applicable. Culture is the orbit wherein human beings can live according to their best natures. Cultural anthropology, the study of both humanity and human culture, adopts a multifaceted approach and has an important role to play in the future. My discussions with you have reinforced my conviction that this is true.

Yalman: Yes, leaders today must have the inventiveness to learn lessons from cultural anthropology.

Ikeda: An important point. In its early phase, cultural anthropology investigated surviving primitive cultures on the basis of preconceived notions about what it means to be advanced or backward, civilized or barbarian. Later, however, cultural anthropologists left their desks and went out into the field to study actual primitive lifestyles, languages and tools.

Their efforts triumphed over prejudice as they came to see that all cultures deserve equal respect.

Yalman: Yes. Indeed, cultural anthropology has contributed greatly to the breaking down of prejudices about what is advanced or undeveloped, civilized or barbarian. I am deeply impressed by the keen way in which you go directly to the essential characteristics of anthropology and the fundamental problems it faces.

Ikeda: I understand that, for fieldworkers, local peoples become more than mere objects of study. Anthropologists live side by side with them for extended periods and sometimes form deep friendships with them.

Yalman: Once a researcher begins living with people and learning their languages, tools and lifestyles, enduring friendships develop. In this sense, fieldwork turns out to be one of life's formative experiences.

Sri Lanka

Yalman: My time in Sri Lanka was certainly an absolutely critical experience in my own intellectual and personal development. It is true that, coming from Istanbul, I found myself in a highly alien atmosphere. It was not the first time. Earlier in England, I had to come to terms with an alien culture – the British at home. But England was not totally unfamiliar because, after all, Istanbul is very much a European city as well as an Asian one. And, in England, too, I made friends who have remained with me ever since.

Ikeda: Profound encounters become treasured parts of our personal histories.

Yalman: Sri Lanka was something else. It involved Buddhism and Hinduism and intimate relationships with people in small villages. Some lived according to Buddhism; in the Hindu districts, people were concerned with their gods and rituals. Sri Lanka provided experiences that are hard to replicate. They had a profound effect on me. The more I spoke with and learned about the Sri Lankans, the more I found myself respecting their viewpoints. Buddhism in particular, with its extraordinary civilization and great intellectual brilliance, had a permanent effect on my thinking. Before going to Sri Lanka, I had never suspected the degree to which a great tradition like Buddhism could affect me and change my attitude about life in general and culture in particular.

Ikeda: I have visited Sri Lanka twice (in 1961 and 1964) and made many friends there. I have conducted a dialogue with the astronomer Dr Chandra Wickramasinghe who, though now living in Britain, was born in Sri Lanka. From my youth, I have been aware of the Buddhist spirit that is vibrantly alive there.

At the San Francisco Peace Conference in 1951, the Sri Lankan delegate spoke of Japanese bombings and exploitation during the Second World War. Then he renounced claims for reparations from Japan by citing Shakyamuni's philosophy that hatred cannot be eliminated through hatred. We Japanese are indebted to him for these words.

Yalman: A noble sentiment. Sri Lanka has an unusual mixture of very intellectual and high-level Theravada Buddhist thought and a long history of lively debate on Buddhism and its significance for the modern world.

Ikeda: Certainly it is impossible to reduce Sri Lanka's Buddhism to a standardized form.

Yalman: Yes, diversity is one of its main characteristics.

Ikeda: Since little of it was transmitted to Japan, Theravada Buddhism remains largely unknown among the Japanese. It did, however, take root on the Asian continent, where it has played an important culture-cultivating role.

Although it is generally regarded as highly traditional in its outlook, I understand that today in places like Sri Lanka, working with non-governmental organizations, Theravada Buddhism actively addresses various contemporary social issues.

Yalman: With its tradition of extremely lively debate, Sri Lankan Buddhism has influenced all kinds of people, including large numbers of Europeans who have come to Sri Lanka to become Buddhists. Some Buddhists – monks mainly – pursue courses of strict training, others follow alternative traditions incorporating local gods and goddesses and the rituals associated with them.

Ikeda: In other words, though native to India, Buddhism in Sri Lanka has melded with local culture in diverse ways.

Yalman: That is true. When I first worked there, I was struck by the opposition between strict Buddhism and local religions. The more educated people adopted an intellectual approach towards Buddhism. Villagers and peasantry, on the other hand, were much more utilitarian. They were interested in serving gods and getting rid of demons. This, too, is very understandable, very human.

Ikeda: Your discovery recalls ideas Claude Lévi-Strauss expresses in his *The Savage Mind*. According to him, we must not indiscriminately call other societies retarded or primitive. If we carefully and closely examine them, we can discover rational significance behind their actions. For example, acts that seem primitive may actually be attempts to restore human relations between distressed people and their associates.

For the self and others

Yalman: Yes. Careful examination revealed to me the meanings of ceremonies that initially seemed uncivilized. Sri Lanka provided a whole series of such discoveries that profoundly enriched my understanding of the human condition.

Ikeda: We must always avoid misunderstandings, prejudices and preconceived evaluations. Tsunesaburo Makiguchi cautioned against evaluating without understanding. The first step must be to examine the facts candidly and with an open mind.

Yalman: In Sri Lanka, I learned that people in different stations in life have different needs and different ways of approaching religion. Discovering this certainly enlarged my own awareness of religious experience. I was moved to understand the immense contribution that Buddhism has made to the general human situation. That experience has remained with me.

Ikeda: A wonderful experience. The influence it exerts on real life is an essential aspect of religion. The *kanji* character for *shū* in *shūkyō*, the Japanese word for religion, means 'the essence'. The real value of religion is its ability to flow from root-like foundations through human beings and their society, and to branch out and blossom throughout the cosmos.

Buddhism teaches us to build a realm of happiness, not for the self alone, but also for others. In the Buddhist scripture called the Srimala Sutra, Queen Srimala expresses her intention of making great gain, not for herself, but for the suffering, defenceless poor. Nichiren wrote, 'Joy means that oneself and others together experience joy.'[1]

Buddhism also teaches us the importance of sublimating our purposes to higher ideas instead of merely rejecting and suppressing desires: '... they are burning the firewood of earthly desires, summoning up the wisdom fire of bodhi or enlightenment.'[2]

The need for dialogue

Yalman: My Sri Lanka experience changed me in yet another way. As I said, the people there adhere to many different forms of faith, and religious organizations are very active. There are many Roman Catholics, Muslims and people from different castes.

Ikeda: Yes, I know. On my first visit, because we arrived at night, I failed to notice this. But the next day I saw that our lodgings were next door to a mosque where services were underway. I was especially struck by this because I had always thought of Sri Lanka as a Buddhist country.

Yalman: It was not very easy to establish communication between different religious groups there. They all remained quite separate, and related to each other only at a basic group level. The lack of intellectual exchange led me to think about the need for more serious levels of dialogue.

Ikeda: Dialogue is indeed the important thing. We must avoid religious clashes. But we must not let differences serve as reasons for isolation and segregation, which only create barriers. Because I know that we must create circuits of exchange, for years I have engaged in dialogues with many different people of various religious, cultural and ideological backgrounds.

Yalman: The kind of dialogue needed in Sri Lanka is precisely the kind you have always conducted. It is the kind you and I are now participating in. Such dialogues are very valuable in establishing serious intellectual communication on the ethical and moral plane between different religious traditions. And for that I am very grateful.

Good relations

Ikeda: To change the subject slightly, I should like to tell a story that provides food for thought on the topic of good relations with others. The research worker Masaaki Noda of Kwansei Gakuin University places great value on sound fieldwork. A psychopathologist who researches mental illness in many parts of the world, he says that, whenever possible, he does fieldwork alone – without the disruption compatriots would inevitably introduce.

To discover why he feels this way, let us imagine two Japanese people conducting a survey in a village in New Guinea. As they work, they naturally converse in Japanese, with the result that the people they are studying regard them as outsiders. This sets up a kind of 'us and them' barrier.

Yalman: I raise both hands in agreement with Mr Noda. The more people of your own culture you have around you, the more likely you are to live in a bubble. The more people who speak to you in your own language, the more you are cut off from local people.

Ikeda: Of course, Mr Noda draws up plans beforehand, listens to advisers and relies on interpreters' assistance. He could possibly tolerate one or two people hanging around. But for him person-to-person contact with the locals, not with compatriots, is crucial. In many cases, lone travellers unfamiliar with the local geography are readily accepted and aided, whereas a large group might be considered a threat.

Yalman: Anthropologists must adopt the same attitude as Mr Noda. It is really very important for them to open themselves up individually and be alone in other cultures, in which they then become immersed. It sinks into their pores, like the water of a hot Japanese bath. So here again, you have really put your finger on the critical issue.

79

A brilliant Norwegian anthropologist, Fredrik Barth, once told me that, when working in a tiny, faraway community deep in New Guinea (the Baktaman), he adopted the local habit of always going barefoot. He said that walking gingerly barefoot on a slippery log placed across a rushing stream alone in the jungle helped him empathize with the circumstances in which the locals lived. The unusual experience brought him much closer to the people and culture around him.

Ikeda: The attitude we are describing goes beyond scholarly fieldwork and is applicable to fundamental topics transcending racial and religious differences. The important issue is approaching others on the basis of our shared humanity. Conflict often arises when encounters are dominated by racial and religious differences, but dialogue results when people come together on the common ground of membership of the human race. True religious dialogues also occur on the basis of person-to-person encounters. Indeed the condition for true religious dialogue is personal contact and the search for breakthroughs between two parties, both of whom share the common suffering caused by birth, ageing, sickness and death.

Developing empathy

Yalman: The person-to-person contact you mention is a topic of great interest to me. Lévi-Strauss considered empathy the key sentiment in human relations. He referred to Jean-Jacques Rousseau's concept of empathy and sympathy with others' sorrows and joys. You are returning to that same idea. I would agree that empathy is the hallmark of true humanity. It must be developed and can only evolve through person-to-person exchanges. As you point out, one of the missions of religion is to improve the quality of our exchanges and bind human beings of diverse cultural and social backgrounds closer together. That perception is certainly to be supported and underlined.

Ikeda: Mention of developing empathy reminds me of a famous passage in the *Mahavagga* of the *Vinaya Pitaka*, where Shakyamuni instructs his disciples to move with empathy among the people one by one, never in twos, for the sake of their interest and comfort. This relates to what was said earlier about person-to-person encounters. Shakyamuni himself follows his own instruction when he goes, alone, to teach at Uruvela Sena village. In going abroad singly to engage in their teaching work, Shakyamuni and his disciples were expressing the leonine spirit of the person of faith who stands alone, accepting all responsibility. Their actions can also be interpreted as developing fundamental human relationships with others on a person-to-person basis, free of all the structures that breed antagonism.

Yalman: I am in full agreement. I might add that Islam rejects monasticism and priestly orders for this reason. The learned man (*alim*) must go among the people, marry and have children, work and trade in the market like them, but remain conscious of his (or her) high ethical calling at all times. Structured social methods are instruments of alienation.

Ikeda: Those arrogant people in the religious world who, while putting themselves in a safe place to escape from the challenges facing humankind, despise the ordinary people, are just abandoning their noble mission. We of the Soka Gakkai have been fighting against parochial religious authority represented by such people. Although all of us must face ageing, illness and death, our revulsion against these inevitabilities breeds aversion towards the old, the ill and the dead. In the sutra collection called the *Anguttara-nikāya*, reflection on the way in which human beings become arrogant about youth, health and vitality is said to have been what prompted Shakyamuni to pursue the path to truth. It was also the origin of his empathy with the sufferings of others.

Today we might add two additional arrogances to the list. First, out of desire to avoid poverty, the arrogance of wealth breeds contempt for poor people and impoverished countries. Second, the arrogance of the majority, which, out of insecurity in the face of the possibility of persecution, breeds dislike for minorities.

Yalman: The concern Prince Siddhartha demonstrates in relation to old age, illness and death is indeed an example of the great humanism of the Buddhist tradition. To this day, we have found no answers to these age-old issues. The only way to approach the matter is through a sense of empathy and support for people who are suffering. In that respect, the points you make about Buddhism are very pertinent.

The age of soft power

Yalman: You have delivered two wonderful addresses at Harvard University: 'The Age of Soft Power' in 1991, and 'Mahayana Buddhism and the Twenty-First-Century Civilization' in 1993, which I heard.

Ikeda: I shall never forget the great assistance you provided on that occasion.

Yalman: Your idea of 'The Age of Soft Power' is far-reaching and important. The shortcomings of hard power can be disastrous, as in the aftermath of the terrorist attacks on the United States on September 11, 2001. In my opinion, it was a great mistake for the United States to resort to hard power after 9/11. It is not that I recommend making no response at all, but 9/11 should have been treated as a criminal, not a military, act. It was not warfare – it was a crime. Attempts to use hard, military power in Afghanistan and Iraq caused a great many local deaths. Far from stimulating recognition and gratitude, American actions had a very negative effect. Pakistan was destabilized, and Central Asia became much more problematic than before. The Arab world seethed with repressed anger and confusion. Muslims in many parts of the world, who had been relatively open and sympathetic to lofty American promises of equality and liberty, became cynical and alienated. The depressing nightmares of Guantánamo and Abu Ghraib will not be easily exorcised.

It could all have been avoided. It would have been much more effective to use the immense soft power of the United States to bring to bear on the idea of justice and fairness in these countries. Diplomatic work would have been much more effective. If the United States had used its expertise in the Western countries along with the United Nations, the world would have been a much safer place today.

Ikeda: Sadly, what you say is entirely true. And that is precisely why we must persevere in convincing people that dialogue is the only road to peace. With utter determination, we must build new peace relations for the twenty-first century.

Yalman: As you indicate, soft power, effectively used, would have been, in my opinion, a better way to go. I am very much attached to Gandhi's idea that ends do not justify means.

Ikeda: I agree. Gandhi opposed the notion that violent means must be used to attain righteous ends. Peace can only be achieved through peaceful means. Gandhi proclaimed this and his widespread non-violence movement was consistent with his proclamation. We must learn from his example.

Yalman: The nature of the means employed determines the character of the ends achieved. This is certainly true for the United States' foreign policy.

Ikeda: Although it might seem a more roundabout way – and in the face of criticisms of impotence from all quarters – I believe the only path to world security in the twenty-first century is to improve the competence of the United Nations. After all, it came into being as a result of lessons learned from the tragedies of two world conflicts in the twentieth century.

SEVEN

Reviving Asian Humanism

Equal dignity

Yalman: Today we must avoid isolated religionism and build an open, wholesome, contemporary secularism that willingly respects all the great ethical teachings of diverse religious traditions. This is what I mean when I speak of *humanism*. Different cultures and religions will have a common ground for dialogue only after we establish this kind of generous and informed humanism.

Ikeda: I agree. The philosophy of dialogue that, transcending religion and ideology, is humanistic in nature is absolutely essential. I have many friends in the world of Islam. For instance, I have held talks with Abdurrahman Wahid, former president of the Republic of Indonesia, and conducted profound exchanges with Prince El Hassan bin Talal of Jordan, who is a former president of the Club of Rome. I have published a dialogue with Professor Majid Tehranian. And now, I am engaged in this important dialogue with you.

Yalman: Religions that remain isolated have no future. All religions must respect and learn from each other. Each one has important and different insights into the human condition gathered over long centuries. In spite of the efforts of people like yourself, who work to break down barriers between them, I am apprehensive about the crisis facing humanism today in both Asia and the West. One major aspect of the crisis is the refusal of modern civilization to come to terms with death as well as with the industries of death. You discussed this in one of your Harvard lectures.

Ikeda: The awareness of death – and thus of the finite nature of our existence – transcends animal instinct and makes human life more fulfilled. The formulation of a firm view of life and death, therefore, is vital to enabling us to live in ways suitable to our humanity. Mahayana Buddhism expounds joy in both life and death. In our discussion of this topic, Professor Toynbee expressed great concern over the modern tendency to turn away from death and fail to prepare for the end.

Yalman: Preoccupation with Hollywood-style youth culture pretends that death does not exist. Adherents of this culture simply forget about the end of life. Their approach is the opposite of what Prince Siddhartha experienced in his confrontations of birth, ageing, illness and death, and of what he concluded after becoming a Buddha.

Ikeda: Thinking that life, with its repetitive cycles of novelties, information and pleasure, goes on forever is delusional. No matter how we try to ignore it, death is inevitable.

Yalman: In its ceaseless preoccupation with self-improvement and consumerism, modern civilization perpetuates the false view that life will last forever. In the frenetic striving for wealth and acquisitions, people appear to be oblivious to the ancient Muslim saying that 'shrouds do not have pockets.' You cannot take it all with you.

Ikeda: This attitude creates aversion for the aged, the sick and the dead. Shakyamuni severely criticized such aversion as arrogance.

Yalman: There is no other word for it. Such arrogance makes people willing to sacrifice the lives of others so long as they can protect their own. Ignoring death allows the development of horrific instruments of death such as nuclear weapons, the horrendous destructive force of which we witnessed in the last century. We have not yet come to terms with the significance of what this means from the viewpoint of the future of civilization.

Ikeda: That is precisely why we must vigorously promote respect for life. Buddhist philosophy concentrates on uncovering the arrogance that generates aversion for others and discovering the ultimate dignity inherent in all forms of life.

Yalman: Aversion towards others corresponds to the obsession with differences that you discussed in one of the messages you delivered at Harvard. Today, in many supposedly liberal countries, this obsession, combined with xenophobia, is reaching levels of mass public hysteria.

Ikeda: Shakyamuni repeatedly insisted that we stop being obsessed with differences. The Mahayana bodhisattva lives in such a way as to do this. While seeking to eliminate his own suffering, the bodhisattva works to save others from suffering. This indeed is the nature of the bodhisattva. The bodhisattva idea of harmonious symbiosis and universal prosperity is extremely important now, when the world is rife with fictitious distinctions like those between industrialized and industrializing nations, civilized and undeveloped individuals, democracies and tyrannies.

Yalman: Precisely so. The bodhisattva is an example of how fundamental human relationships should be.

Ikeda: Commenting on a speech I delivered at Claremont McKenna College in 1993, Linus Pauling made some memorable points. He said that, by sincerely extending the hand of salvation to people in distress, the bodhisattva bears witness to the beauty of humanity and provides a key to creating ties of sympathy that transcend divisions. He added that the essential and vital role of religions is to contribute to peace and to save suffering, ordinary people.

Yalman: Linus Pauling, the father of modern chemistry and twice a Nobel laureate, was a most admirable person. I knew him and his brilliant son Peter – also a distinguished physicist – and his lovely daughter Linda from my days with them at Cambridge University, at the exciting time when the mystery of DNA was being deciphered. I am in complete agreement with his comments.

Ikeda: I met with Dr Pauling for discussions four times in the United States. All the meetings were impressive and memorable. He was a man with a warm and big heart. In order to trace his distinguished life and influence, we of the Soka Gakkai International, with co-sponsorship from the Pauling family and Oregon State University, have held the exhibition 'Linus Pauling and the Twentieth Century' in many places over the world – including the United States, Japan and Europe. I have had several occasions to talk with Dr Pauling Jr, chairperson of the exhibition advisory committee and the chairperson of the Board of Trustees for the Linus Pauling Institute of Science and Medicine.

Yalman: I feel honoured to be able to pay homage to his memory.

Diversity and symbiosis in the Ottoman Empire

Ikeda: The lessons we can learn from Islamic history can help us promote harmonious coexistence and mutual prosperity for the whole human race. More specifically, Ottoman history shows the empire to have been admirable in numerous respects, as is illustrated by the manner in which Constantinople was taken over. The Turks allowed the indigenous people to preserve their traditional customs and rites without interference. They were permitted to travel freely at home and abroad on commercial business. Their sons were not drafted into the Janissaries (infantrymen in the sultan's guard), and no one was compelled to convert to Islam. Indeed, one of the first and most far-reaching acts of the sultan (Mehmet) was to ensure the continuity and legitimacy of the Greek Orthodox Church. The diverse Christian peoples in the empire, both in the Balkans and in the East, were thereby invited into the fold.

Yalman: The Ottomans were a remarkable dynasty. As you point out, they did not force anyone to convert to Islam. People of different religions were able to continue their practices without interference. The empire provided a very welcome haven for Jews escaping racism and the destruction of the Jewish way of life in Spain and other parts of Western Europe. They found a peaceful home in the Ottoman Empire. Famous letters from the sixteenth and seventeenth centuries by Jews in the empire urged their co-religionists in Germany and France to join them. Some of these letters still exist. The gist of the letters was that they promised lives of safety, personal and religious freedom, and happiness in Turkey.

Bernard Lewis quotes the famous Edirne letter 'written some time in the first half of the fifteenth century':

> I have heard of the afflictions, more bitter than death, that have befallen our brethren in Germany – of the tyrannical laws, the compulsory baptisms and the banishments, which are of daily occurrence . . . on all sides I learn of anguish of soul and torment of body; . . . Brothers and teachers, friends and acquaintances! I,

> Isaac Zarfati, though I spring from a French stock, yet I was born in Germany, and sat there at the feet of my esteemed teachers. I proclaim to you that Turkey is a land wherein nothing is lacking, and where, if you will, all shall be well with you. The way to the Holy Land lies open to you through Turkey . . . Here every man may dwell at peace under his own vine and fig tree. Here you are allowed to wear the most precious garments. In Christendom, on the contrary, you dare not even venture to clothe your children in red or in blue, according to your taste, without exposing them to the insult of beaten black and blue, or kicked green and red, and therefore are ye condemned to go about meanly clad in sad colored raiment . . . and now, seeing all these things, O Israel, wherefore sleepest thou? Arise! And leave this accursed land forever.

Lewis goes on to quote from a Portuguese Jew a century later, Samuel Usque: 'most signal [among the human consolations] is great Turkey, a broad and spacious sea which God opened with the rod of His mercy as He opened the Red Sea at the time of the exodus . . . here the gates of liberty are always open for the observance of Judaism.' and adds, 'this must have come as a considerable surprise to a traveller from sixteenth century Portugal.'[1]

It is a matter of great regret that subtle – and not so subtle – racism, which led to the destruction of the Jews and their displacement to Israel, is now practised against Muslim immigrants in a supposedly chastened and enlightened Europe. The European Union, which prides itself on its liberality, has, in fact, much to learn from the open-mindedness of the early Ottomans.

Ikeda: The name of Constantinople was changed to Istanbul, which became the capital. But, even at the height of imperial power, the population of the city is estimated to have been sixty per cent Muslim and forty per cent non-Muslim.

Yalman: Just so. The impartiality of your views is impressive. In the United States, prejudices against the Chinese, Japanese, Arabs and Muslims were very evident until recent times. It is not so long ago that the Chinese in San Francisco and Los Angeles were denied the vote. But recently things have changed – nowadays people of Asian background are very welcome and extremely successful in America. This does not mean that there are no movements against them, that there is no resentment in certain areas. But, on the whole, most elements of American society have been extremely welcoming, open-minded and accepting of religious diversity.

Ikeda: I am one of those who love American magnanimity. Respect and tolerance towards diversity are key to social prosperity.

Yalman: I agree. Still, I am uneasy about the rise of Christian fundamentalism and evangelism in America. Europe increasingly demonstrates intense Islamophobia, evident in the reactions to the Muslim outrage at Danish cartoons mocking the Prophet. After 9/11, the mood in the United States also turned extremely suspicious – especially towards persons of Arab descent, and towards other Muslims and Islam in general. It is to be hoped that this witch-hunting climate will be a passing phenomenon, as McCarthyism was.

We must return to the culture of tolerance, acceptance, understanding and empathy and disavow baser passions associated essentially with a sense of self-importance and paranoia; that is, with both individual aggrandizement and fear of what enemies might do. We must not allow xenophobic feelings to get the upper hand. As it sets so important an example for the rest of the world, the United States must demonstrate responsible leadership in this regard.

Cultural enrichment

Ikeda: In our dialogue, Professor Majid Tehranian of the University of Hawaii spoke of a lack of familiarity with Islamic culture among the people of Japan. Unfortunately, Japan demonstrates the informational biases about Islam that Edward Said pointed out in *Covering Islam*. Nonetheless, Islamic culture influences our daily lives. For instance, many things and words in daily use are Islamic or Arab in origin: pyjamas, cotton, sofa, magazine, lemon, orange, syrup and tulip are but a few examples. Even the football-match cheer *Olé Olé*! is said to derive from an Arabic expression meaning 'from God'. Numerous elements like these have had culturally enriching effects all over the world. This extensive Islamic cultural heritage enriches our daily lives and demonstrates the importance Islam can have in our lives.

Yalman: Your pronouncements on Islam are always appropriate. It is wonderful to talk with you about the positive aspects of Islam in a Buddhist context, and to bring Soka Gakkai into closer focus with the practical aspects of Islam. I think Mahatma Gandhi, whom I respect greatly, had the right idea when he said that their positive teachings really do bring the world's great religions together. Insufficient understanding of their own true natures, however, sometimes leads their followers astray.

Ikeda: Your insight is very significant. Conflicts arise more from political and economic causes than from religious confrontations. The struggle between Israel and Palestine and the Middle East policies of the United States government make this perfectly apparent.

Islamic culture

Ikeda: There are 1.3 billion Muslims in the world today – more than one-fifth of the global population. Knowledge of Islamic culture is therefore essential to any consideration of world events. Indeed, ignorance of it constitutes a cause for unnecessary antagonism.

While being strict with its own believers, Islam exerts no compulsion on believers of other faiths. Is it true that this attitude is clearly enjoined by the Koran?

Yalman: Yes. This is a very important issue. If there is one element that can be singled out as the most prominent aspect of Islam, I would say that it is a sense of respect for the individual spirit and the individual soul.

Ikeda: Such respect relates to tolerance, which itself is a mainstay of democracy.

Yalman: I agree. It expresses itself in immense support for the idea of equality. That, in a sense, is one of the most significant elements of Islam, in contradistinction to many other world religions. It is also painfully true, however, that the ideals of equality (and democracy) are far from being realized, in political terms, in far too many Islamic states.

Ikeda: I understand that Islam has religious scholars and leaders (*ulema*), but no priesthood.

Yalman: That is true. The word *ulema* is the plural of *alim* – a learned person. Other religions always recognize a priestly or monastic elite. Basically Islam rejects the idea of privileged access to a higher piety. It is the individual that counts, so equality is a key element. In fact, Sayyid Abul A'la Maududi (1903–79), a radical Islamist thinker from Pakistan, was speaking of equality as a major element when he said that, to understand the nature of Islam, one should visit Mao Zedong's China.

Ikeda: Professor Tehranian told me that alms giving (*zakat*), one of the pillars of Islam, is a tangible expression of the emphasis on equality. It effects a redistribution of wealth by using contributions to help the poor, the distressed and the indebted, and to free slaves.

Yalman: Yes. The idea of justice and fairness is very important because equality is always expressed in Islam in a community context. The sense of community is key – within the community, the sense of equality and the intentions of the individual are emphasized, in what amounts to a return to the inner psychological aspects of kindness and goodness.

Ikeda: A society based on equality can come into existence only as a result of mutually positive intentions. In 2004, on the occasion of my receiving an honorary doctorate in humanities from the University of Jordan, His Highness Prince El Hassan bin Talal of Jordan sent me a most courteous message, in which he mentioned the Islamic spirit of competition in mutual beneficence. A century ago, Tsunesaburo Makiguchi said that instead of military and economic competition, humanity should turn its attention to humanitarian competition.

Yalman: Another very important Islamic concept is the application of reason (*aql*) and self-control. In this respect, Islam is a very modern religion – quite appropriate to contemporary society. It calls for equality, social justice, fairness in all dealings and the application and acceptance of reason. In doing this, it calls for the acceptance of science as well.

Ikeda: Islamic science flourished between the eighth and fifteenth centuries. In later times, the emphasis in Islam shifted towards religious matters, as the West – ironically on the basis of knowledge provided by Islamists – experienced the scientific revolution of the seventeenth century and took the lead in further scientific developments. Numerous chemical terms such as *alkali* and *alcohol*, both derived from Arabic, bear witness to Islamic influence.

Divine love

Yalman: Yet another very important element distinguishing it from some of the other world religions is Islam's immense emphasis on the idea of divine love. For centuries, literature in the Urdu, Punjabi, Persian, Turkish and Arabic traditions has been about the individual's love of God. Centuries of writing, particularly poetry, deal with the love of the individual for God, which is really a metaphor for the love of human beings for each other. This is a critical matter because obviously the great Islamic poets and writers have emphasized the expansion of love from the individual towards the entire community.

Ikeda: A symbol of Islamic humanism.

Yalman: Yes. Other traditions also emphasize the idea of love. For instance, I might mention the Gopis and their unconditional devotion to Krishna in the Indian *bhakti* tradition.

As a human being, Jesus expressed Christian love for the rest of the world. In Buddhism, Maitreya – the Buddha of the future – embodies compassion.

Ikeda: Maitreya, whose name in Sanskrit means friendly or amicable, symbolizes compassionate activity. But he is not always as gentle as a spring breeze. To correct people's mistakes he may sometimes speak in words of flame. Nichiren Buddhism teaches that the compassion of Maitreya means acting like a parent in order to turn people away from evil.

Yalman: That is a very righteous philosophy. In Islam, the idea of divine love expressed in human metaphors and human terms is developed to an extraordinary extent. Otherwise, we would not have had such an immense outpouring of feeling and emotion on the subject. In all Islamic countries, from the eighth century to the present, the great Sufi traditions have been closely associated with the sense of adoration for other human beings, which of course underlines the desire for peace and acceptance. Writings in this tradition represent an early recognition of individual illumination, which is a metaphor for individual human rights.

Ikeda: One of the luminaries of that tradition is the Persian Sufi poet Jalal al-Din Rumi. Located in Konya, in central Turkey, his tomb bears an inscribed invitation to all people to come to that place.

Yalman: The great mystic saint Rumi personified the concept of love. Stories about him highlight how the teachings of many generations of Islamic saints stress affection and empathy. For instance, once a group of Greek Orthodox monks met him in the royal city of Konya. They saluted him very respectfully, and he in turn saluted them in the same fashion. They repeated their salute; and he did the same, bowing even deeper to express his appreciation of their goodness and kindness.

When Rumi died, after a life devoted to teaching human decency, the whole town of Konya celebrated his union with God. Members of all communities – Christians, Jews and others – came together to commemorate his achievements and his life.

Ikeda: Rumi's way of life went beyond religious and ethnic differences. We can all learn a great deal from it. His bowing in response to the greeting he received from the Orthodox monks illustrates the mutual respect we should all have for the life force inherent in each of us. The Buddhist scriptures employ a lovely metaphor to symbolize such reciprocal respect: when a person bows to a reflection in a mirror, the reflection bows in return.[2]

Yalman: The profound interest you demonstrate in the force of life during your dialogue with Linus Pauling underscores the need to make the twenty-first a century devoted to the celebration of life. How right you are. We are now on the brink of great peril caused by immense tensions and lethal passions unleashed by short-sighted, arrogant policies on the international stage.

We are all hostages to the people with their fingers on the nuclear buttons around the world. If they make a wrong decision, the world will be a much sorrier place; and life on this planet will be devastated.

Ikeda: Very true. Nuclear weapons are the antipode of respect for life. My mentor Josei Toda described nuclear weapons as an absolute evil. He said this in the proclamation he made entrusting the task of ridding the world of such weaponry to me and his other disciples. Half a century has passed since that declaration, but it is with me in everything I do.

In his own energetic struggle for the abolition of nuclear weapons, Linus Pauling expected a great deal from grass roots peace movements because he believed that ordinary people have the power to set politicians on the right path.[3]

Yalman: Buddhist respect for life in all its manifestations is laudable and critically important. We need the kindness of *ahimsa* – not taking life – now more than ever before.

Ikeda: Buddhism expounds the dignity of life. It is founded on the world view set forth in the doctrine of dependent origination – according to which, all life is interrelated and interdependent. All life forms are eternally connected throughout the entire cosmos – from the infinite past, through the present, to the infinite future. Nor is the relationship static. Each individual is influenced by their social environment and is capable of self-reform. Each inspires every other individual to strive for the mutual joy of all. That is why Buddhism regards killing as the most serious offence and expounds *ahimsa*.

Yalman: In the Islamic interpretation, life is always celebrated, not only for the individual and their own interests, but also always in the context of society. The community is critical.

But this interpretation runs completely counter to basic

elements of American pop culture, in which egotism – epitomized by the so-called 'me' generation – is celebrated, with very negative results from the viewpoint of public life. This kind of egotism supports the culture of violence associated with guns. Congress has already allowed gun manufacturers and dealers too much freedom – as if there were not already enough weapons around! All this relates to a lack of respect for human life – a cheapening of human life, and emphasis on the vigilante mindset.

Ikeda: In speaking of exchanges between Turkey and Japan, you once stated the need to create a forum for mutual exchanges between our countries, a place where we can revive and rebuild the great Asian humanism represented by sages from Shakyamuni Buddha to Rumi. You added that it would be a shining example for cooperation, not only in Asia, but also on all continents – in the name of building peace, prosperity, freedom, humaneness and civilization.

The Buddhist and Islamic philosophies of harmonious coexistence and respect for life can lead the whole world towards prosperity. Today distrust of humanity and cheapening of life are becoming increasingly widespread. To halt them we must rebuild and propagate the great Asian philosophy of humanism. I am convinced that our dialogue can contribute substantially to that endeavour.

EIGHT

Global Governance

_____

The United Nations

Ikeda: In February 2006, to commemorate the tenth anniversary of its founding, the Toda Institute for Global Peace and Policy Research held a highly fruitful conference in Los Angeles on the topic 'Transforming the United Nations'. Among the peace activists attending were Anwarul K. Chowdhury, UN Under-Secretary-General; Ved Nanda, University of Denver vice-provost; and David Krieger, president of the Nuclear Age Peace Foundation. The meeting, which addressed issues such as human development, regional conflicts and global governance, provided a venue for forecasting the nature of the UN and for seeking ways to reform and strengthen it.

In proposals I made in January 2006, to commemorate Soka Gakkai International Day, I called for the creation of a United Nations devoted to the interests of the ordinary people of the world. In a similar vein, many people attending the conference cited the need for reforms focused, not on nations, but on all humanity.

Yalman: I have had the honour of participating in several Toda Institute projects, including the international conference on 'Dialogue of Civilizations' held in Okinawa in 2000. I hope that the institute will continue contributing to peace through its profoundly significant and creative activities and that I may have a part in them.

From destruction to creativity

Ikeda: Thank you for your deep understanding and warm words. The late Joseph Rotblat, who was president emeritus of the Pugwash Conferences, delivered the keynote speech at the Okinawa conference you attended. The essence of his memorable address was the creation of a world free of nuclear weapons and war.

On that occasion, he and I discussed the realization of such a world. Later he spoke of his wish to tell young people, who will be responsible for the future, about the pacific mindset. We also started a serial dialogue in a monthly magazine on the occasion of the fiftieth anniversary of the Russell–Einstein Manifesto. He devoted himself completely to the project right up until shortly before his death. I am certain that the dialogues will convey his message of peace to the young people of the world and that they will take up the task inherent in it.

Yalman: I agree. His death was a great loss. When I met him in Okinawa, I was deeply impressed by his strong faith in peace.

I was equally impressed to see how Professor Majid Tehranian and representatives of diverse philosophical backgrounds, including Christian, Islamic, Jewish, Buddhist and Hindu faiths, took part in the conference on the vital issue of intercultural exchanges. To be frank, at first I wondered whether people of such diverse backgrounds would be able to confer together in a meaningful way. But my worries proved unfounded. With deep mutual understanding, they eagerly sought ways to put their wisdom to use in addressing contemporary problems.

Ikeda: Since its very inception, the Toda Institute has consistently stressed intercultural dialogues. Based on the advice of Professor Tehranian, who is Iranian by birth, coupled with its own assessment of the world trend, the government of Iran proposed to the UN General Assembly that 2001 be designated the 'Year of Dialogue among Civilizations'. Tragically, however, the events of 11 September 2001 involved acts of indiscriminate terrorism that are the diametric opposite of dialogue.

Yalman: Deep racism and formidable political errors in the Middle East lie at the heart of terrorist acts like those of 9/11. Dialogues resulting in correct understanding of other races and cultures are essential to severing the roots of such violence. Both East and West have much to learn from their mistakes.

In post-9/11 America, though misunderstanding and prejudice towards Islam run rife, some young people are still striving to understand people of different backgrounds better. For instance, students queued in the corridors to attend a course of lectures entitled 'Thought and Change in the Modern Middle East' that I delivered at Harvard. In the lecture hall, some had to stand; others sat on the floor. I later learned that a number of the students attending had lost their fathers in the World Trade Center collapse.

Ikeda: Young people like those who strive to understand other cultures are a ray of light in an increasingly dark, fragmented world. In October 2001, the American publisher Rodale issued *From the Ashes, A Spiritual Response to the Attack on America*, messages on the tragedy by seventy prominent thinkers from around the world. In my own contribution to it, I wrote that, in direct opposition to the hatred and destructiveness dividing society, humanity is inherently endowed with living compassion and creativity.

These traits produce invisible fundamental connections, on the basis of which we can change the direction of our age from division to connection and from destruction to creativity.

Yalman: I agree entirely. Nothing can come of the hatred–destruction cycle. I recall very vividly a conference that took place in Istanbul in the summer of 2001. At the meeting, Palestinians and Israelis discussed prospects for peace. The Israeli delegation insisted on very extreme measures, which the Palestinians met with immense hostility. As I listened to the discussion, I remarked to an American friend that these people were unaware of the kind of hostility – the kind of anger and aggression – they were unleashing against each other and that, if this went on, we would be in really serious trouble.

Ikeda: As you foresaw, the Middle East peace process floundered, and an horrendous situation developed in Iraq. Outside the Middle East, too, terrorist attacks against ordinary citizens have occurred in numerous places. For instance, the simultaneous bombings in London during the 2005 G8 summit, and terrorist bombings in Egypt and Bali and elsewhere have taken many lives and caused great misery.

Overcoming fanaticism

Yalman: I am deeply concerned about the fanaticism that dehumanizes and defines the 'other' as the enemy, and that seeks scapegoats. We must do everything we can to increase awareness of the neglected emotional and political problems at the root of terrorist acts.

Ikeda: I agree completely. On the day following the terrorist attacks in the United States, I spoke with Sodovjamtsyn Khurelbaatar, Mongolian ambassador to Japan, who said that human beings ought to de-emphasize nationalism and think in terms of our shared nature as Earthlings. His assertion strengthened my own conviction on this matter.

More than a hundred years ago, Tsunesaburo Makiguchi emphasized the importance of being aware of ourselves as citizens of the world. In his *A Geography of Human Life*, published in 1903, he urged people to avoid narrow-minded nationalism and open themselves up to the whole world as global citizens. Of course, they must also maintain roots in their local districts, which provide the foundations for their daily lives. For Josei Toda, the doctrine of global citizenship for the sake of building a peaceful world, where all races can live in happiness, was an key article of his faith. His goal was nothing less than eliminating the very word *misery*.

Yalman: Both approaches are indispensable. We must devote greater dialogue to resolving the problem of fanaticism.

Jean-Jacques Rousseau said that human beings do not like to see their own kind suffer. He was speaking of empathy, which is the bodhisattva aspect of human beings – the feelings of kindness and love that many religions teach should be directed toward both God and other humans. As we indicated earlier, however, the tendency to define the other as an enemy and a scapegoat is always present and very dangerous. This tribal instinct afflicts everyone.

Ikeda: Lamentably, in ethnic conflicts, religion is frequently used as a means of provoking antagonism and hatred and severing human connections. Repeated over and over in history, this tragedy is often played out against a background of political and economic clashes. One cause of the trouble is the tendency for self-serving, dogmatic religions to treat human beings as tools and make them serve the interests of that religion. This is, of course, an inversion of the true order of things. In cases of this kind, terrorism becomes the suicide of religion.

In its true nature, religion cultivates bonds among people and provides the grounds for a rich spiritual blossoming. Sometimes, however, it betrays this true nature by becoming a hotbed for energies of division and destruction. Twenty-first-century humanity must reverse this mistake and move in a new direction – towards a renaissance of religion. In this regard, people of religious faith bear a heavy responsibility, of which I constantly remind myself.

Facing fear

Yalman: We must be creative in thinking about human experience and make sure it is headed in the right direction – away from fear, of which there is already too much in the world. People are afraid for many reasons: insecurity, their own futures, their economic outlooks. The capitalist world is an unsafe and difficult world where people may be left without jobs and lonely old people without anyone to support them. Even citizens of rich Western countries can find the world a very dangerous and lonely place.

Ikeda: In the insecure world of fear that you describe, I am most concerned about the desperate loneliness of people who, lacking the ethical support and mutual assistance traditionally supplied by family and community bonds, are exposed to various threats and uncertainties about the future. In both the industrialized and developing nations, prevailing conditions make the individual more fragile than ever before. When assailed by spiritual threats, people are left stranded to suffer – as if isolated on a sandbar in the middle of a raging current.

In its pursuit of free individualism, modern civilization has weakened or entirely undone the bonds once provided by family, community and religion. This shakes the very foundation on which the individual stands, thereby casting grave doubts on the maturity of modern civilization. Unless we address the human crisis – the Achilles heel of modern civilization – no amount of material prosperity or techno-scientific progress can ensure world peace or true human advancement.

104

Yalman: That is certainly the case. Modern civilization concentrates too exclusively on technological progress. Hiroshima and Nagasaki, however, have shown that technology by itself is no cause for hope. Progress is not merely a matter of technology – surely it must also include ethical views and lofty goals, such as devotion to improving the world.

Better governance

Ikeda: The legacy of the twentieth century is a war culture of antagonism and destruction. Allowing it to persist unchanged would spell the defeat of humanity. Today the world must employ dialogue and cooperation to build a culture of peace. Achieving this requires solidarity, centred on the United Nations. To prevent further outbreaks of terrorism, we must avoid resorting to military force and reinforce mechanisms for achieving legal solutions through the UN.

Some positive steps in the right direction include the establishment of the International Criminal Court (ICC), the conclusion of the International Convention for the Suppression of Acts of International Terrorism (ICSAIT) and the establishment of specialized UN terrorism-combating bodies. Among them, the ICC opened in 2003 and the ICSAIT was adopted at the UN General Assembly in 2005. Further promising measures I have called for include the creation of a UN committee for the prevention of conflict and a peace-building council. Fortunately, the UN Peace-Building Commission, initiated in late 2005 by the General Assembly, will function like the peace-building council I proposed. I hope it will get up to speed as soon as possible.

Yalman: I am completely in sympathy with your insistence on methods of dealing with terrorism and resolving conflicts that are UN-centred and legal. The way forward must be better governance in the world at large. This means more debates, more discussions and greater involvement of non-Western peoples in their own fates and the future of the world. The stage for the debates must be the United Nations, where China, India, Japan, Middle Eastern countries, Africa and South America will have to play a much greater role.

Ikeda: Of course, the United Nations has its limitations and is subject to criticism. But it is the only organ where most of the nations of the world can participate in what might be called a universal forum of dialogue or an assembly of humanity. That is why we of Soka Gakkai consistently support its activities and why I personally issue annual proposals about reforming and strengthening it. Some of my recent proposals have dealt with the newly established UN Peace-Building Commission and the role of the UN Human Rights Council. My firm conviction is that the Human Rights Council must vigorously champion human-rights education and take measures to prevent human-rights related problems.

Yalman: The continued support you and Soka Gakkai offer for UN actions is very important. The Human Rights Council is an area to which the UN must devote greater attention. We must develop international criminal courts and establish courts of human rights for each region or international criminal courts of a regional kind.

Ikeda: That is a very interesting proposal. I gather you mean establishing regional courts like the European Court of Human Rights.

Yalman: Yes. Setting up regional courts would have a much more immediate and closer impact on the people concerned. Awareness of the existence of a European Court of Human Rights has already had a very positive effect on the Turkish legal system. South-east Asia may need two or three such courts to accommodate cultural differences in areas with sizeable Muslim populations. The same thing is true of Africa. As the southern parts of Africa are culturally very different from the centre, which in turn is very different from the east or west, numerous regional courts will have to be developed.

Courts like this may seem a very ambitious goal, but we have to start somewhere. A good start has been made with the European Court of Human Rights. You are entirely right when you suggest we support such institutions fully. We must work to instil in all people understanding of the need for the rule of law – national as well as international. This is our only hope.

Ikeda: Solving the mountainous accumulation of global problems – including those associated with human rights – requires strengthening the United Nations, regional support structures and local organizations. Working together, the United Nations and local regions can point the way to overcoming the barrier of nationalism that prioritizes national interests. I am certain that this is the road to global governance in the twenty-first century.

NINE

Dialogue: The Magna Carta of Civilization

Sino-Japanese amity

Ikeda: For the sake of further deepening scholarly and educational exchanges between China and Japan, on 6 March 2006, Soka University opened an office in Beijing. I am resolved to work even harder than before for educational exchanges in order to pioneer a path towards a new peace and amity between the two countries.

Yalman: The opening of your Beijing office is truly cause for congratulations. I sincerely hope that, as a new headquarters for educational exchange, it will further strengthen Sino-Japanese relations. This is especially important because amity between Japan and China is vital to the stability of East Asia and world peace in the twenty-first century.

Ikeda: Indeed it is. Wang Xuezhen, former director of the Centre of Japanese Studies of Peking University, was kind enough to accept the position of honorary director. The opening took place while the National People's Congress was in session. Though very busy with the Congress and their work, Chinese officials for foreign affairs and representatives of forty-four Chinese universities and scholarly organizations, the China–Japan Friendship Association, and the All-China Youth Federation attended our ceremonies.

Yalman: Their attendance indicates how deeply the Chinese people trust your organization and what great things they expect from it.

Ikeda: In the spring of 1975, Soka University officially received Chinese students from the new China. It was the first Japanese university to do so. At a meeting I had with him the previous year, Premier Zhou Enlai expressed the hope that Sino-Japanese amity would last for many generations to come. Since that time, Soka University has established connections with more than twenty Chinese universities and has sent or received more than 500 exchange teachers and students. As founder, I was delighted and honoured by the large number of former Soka University Chinese exchange students who attended the opening of the Beijing office. Among them were representatives of the very first group to study with us. They are all now active in various fields in their own country.

Yalman: You have devoted immense time and effort to creating amicable relations with China.

I, too, have become involved with Harvard students who have studied for a year at Peking University – to be followed the next year by Chinese students studying at Harvard. Our ideal is for students to develop relations with universities around the world. The more we introduce our students to their counterparts in other countries, the better we will serve the purposes of the peaceful, decent world we want for the future.

Cosmology based on the dignity of life

Ikeda: Creating such a world is our duty. More than anything, I hope that, through broadening and continuing these exchanges, we will cultivate mutual understanding and develop an awareness of global citizenship in the minds of young people, who bear the burden of the future.

In Chapter Eight, you spoke of fanaticism that defines the other as enemies and scapegoats. I should now like to investigate ways religion can help deal with this problem.

Cultivating respect for life itself is certainly one of those ways. In thought-provoking terms, Claude Lévi-Strauss once remarked that as long as human beings are engrossed in destroying countless life forms, the natural birth of a well-ordered humanism is impossible. He added that it is imperative to put the world ahead of one's own life, all forms of life ahead of humanity alone, and respect for others ahead of personal gain. In the twenty-first century, religions must take this view of the world, of values and of life as their starting point. Religions are urgently required to cultivate an ethos that sends the philosophy of respect for life coursing throughout society.

Yalman: The idea you raise constitutes one of the most wonderful aspects of Lévi-Strauss' work on mythology. He draws attention to the way we human beings create the world around us through our imagination. The mythologies of Buddhism, Islam, Christianity, Jainism, Hinduism, the African religions, Daoism, Sikhism and Judaism are essentially the theoretical creative imagination of people trying to make sense of the world they live in – trying to determine a history and a direction for themselves. They are essentially comparable as elements of human imagination. The creative process of scientific and religious imagination is not all that different. The difference comes in the ethical dimension. Fascinatingly, we are at a turning point in human history in which scientific imagination is much more advanced than religious imagination.

Ikeda: As you point out, the religious mythologies represent efforts to make sense of the world we live in. Modern civilization has concentrated on the development of scientific technology and material prosperity. When we reflect on the loss of spiritual and ethical bases this has caused, we come to see that today humanity requires the restoration of a cosmology created by means of religious imagination. Of course, cosmologies must not be limited to asserting the superiority of one's own group, because this introduces social schism. We require a cosmology that is open to all peoples and that provides the source for respect for the dignity of all life.

Conditions enabling dialogue

Yalman: I have said before that religion has two important aspects. One is the aspect of identity and the other is the aspect of morality and ethics. The identity aspect inspires pride in the foundations of one's faith. It is a kind of tribalism that celebrates the collective spirit. Unfortunately, however, it often causes interfaith conflicts. That is why we must concentrate on the other deeper, spiritual aspect – the moral and ethical sides of religion. This will promote individual self-reform and educate people about building better values for society and future generations. Many religions share spiritual values. Giving them prominence in individual religious identities makes interfaith dialogues possible.

Ikeda: In discussing religion or conducting interfaith dialogue, we must first of all take care not to confuse religiosity with sectarianism. This was a theme of the second address I delivered at Harvard in September 1993. I said that we must reinterpret religions on the criteria of whether they make people stronger or weaker, better or worse, wiser or more foolish.

Yalman: When it loses sight of human communality, the identity aspect of religion can lapse into tribalism, which poses a big problem for the future. The more tribal we are, the more we are inclined to fight with other tribes. Such was the tragic experience of much of the twentieth century – one of the most horrendously violent in human history. As human beings, we exist within collectivities. Our languages create what Durkheim has called a conscience collective. Although it is not something that can be entirely rejected, we must understand the nature of this tribal identity aspect and try to control it.

Ikeda: Very true. Whether a religion has a future depends on whether it manifests the power to encourage and boost the vigorous pursuit of the good and the valuable. Interfaith dialogues founded on our common humanity open paths to the future of religion itself.

Yalman: Yes, they do. The innate and understandable desire to belong to communities must not get out of hand. As I said before, although it is no easy task, the ethical and moral aspects of religion must be brought to the fore.

As the Buddha reminded us, the spirit of empathy, *karuna-metta* – love and pity for living beings – must be rekindled. These are the rocks on which to build a future humanism. Reflecting on Rousseau, Claude Lévi-Strauss has often written in these terms.

Returning to origins

Ikeda: I am certain that Buddhist spirituality has the strength to build the kind of humanism you speak of.

To deal with the task, each religion must return to the spirit of its founder and re-examine itself. Of course, each has its own doctrines. But the founders of all of them anguished over the sufferings of real society and wanted to make people happy. Essentially, returning to their points of origin, religions must empathize with the hardships and sufferings caused by the problems confronting humanity today. Devising ways

113

to eliminate suffering must be the premise on which all their activities are based.

Yalman: That is true. Our duty is not to divide people but to bring them together. That has been the goal of all the great religious leaders of the past. You can see it very clearly in the work of the Buddha, who taught that deeds, not birth, make a person a Brahmin. The prophet Muhammad also tried to use the symbolisms of Judaism, Christianity and Islam to bring people together in a moral community. The words of the Koran to this effect are inscribed around the Dome of the Rock in Jerusalem. We must strive to do the same kind of thing today.

Ikeda: I agree. The world today tends to fragment. We of Soka Gakkai actively undertake intercultural and interfaith dialogues in the hope of building bridges of mutual understanding and friendship to counter this tendency.

For instance, for some years, working with the European Academy of Sciences and Arts, we have been sponsoring the dialogue among four great religions, Christianity, Islam, Judaism and Buddhism. In addition, three research institutions that I founded – the Institute of Oriental Philosophy, the Boston Research Center for the 21st Century and the Toda Institute for Global Peace and Policy Research – have been expanding the network of peace and culture by enthusiastically undertaking intercultural and interfaith dialogues. These are not debates for their own sakes. All of them aim to pool human wisdom to halt conflicts, overcome poverty and prevent further environmental destruction. Without dialogue, human beings are fated to go on travelling in the darkness of self-righteousness. I firmly believe that dialogue is the light that can illumine our steps and help us find the path we ought to follow.

Transcending barren ideological conflicts

Yalman: I agree completely with you when you say that, in a world without dialogue, human beings fall into the darkness of self-righteousness. We must be very aware of the dangers involved in glorifying the separate elements and mythological aspects in religion for people who need some kind of certainty in their lives. That is one of the key problems facing us at the moment. It is an easy task to designate other people as enemies and treat them as scapegoats – to create a false sense of separation and a false sense of danger and paranoia. In all ages, unscrupulous religious preachers have performed this kind of glorification, which, in one instance, led to the great massacres and sufferings of the Crusades. Today the same game is played by politicians who wrap themselves in their national flags and incite the masses to resist perceived enemies. In this process, the media can be turned into a most dangerous instrument of torture and, indeed, war.

Ikeda: Much of the great suffering of the twentieth century, including the inhuman cruelty of the Holocaust, resulted from barren ideological conflicts and the tendency to attribute absolute values to one's own group.

Yalman: Similar tragedies still occur. In recent times the tendency you describe led to terrible events in the former Yugoslavia, where many people were sacrificed when a sense of otherness among groups was overemphasized. People used religious rhetoric to split Catholics from Orthodox Christians and Muslims, even in communities where they all spoke the same language and had basically the same customs. Desperate situations in Palestine, many parts of Africa, the Caucasus and elsewhere persist to this very day. The desperate slaughter between Sunni and Shī'a Muslim Arabs in Iraq should be a warning to the rest of us. Violence breeds terror.

The identity aspect of religion plays a growing role in the world. Catholics are opposed to Greek Orthodox, Jews to

Christians, Muslims to Jews, Hindus to Muslims, Sri Lankan Buddhists to Sri Lankan Hindus, and so on. The result is horrendous murder and killings.

Illuminating civilization with dialogue

Ikeda: Most regrettably and perilously, frequent reports of tragedies caused by religious conflicts are beginning to make some people think that different religions cannot coexist peacefully. Surely this is an issue of major importance.

Yalman: In this regard, we must expand dialogue to the global level, where it can enable religion to provide momentum for the new age. As Jean-Jacques Rousseau wrote in the heady days before the French Revolution of 1789, it is the sentiment of empathy, the feeling of kinship with others, which must be cultivated to make us more human. Otherwise all is lost. Whether a local religion can become a world religion depends on the degree of empathy and understanding it displays towards other cultures. Dialogue is important in cultivating this empathy and understanding because it reveals the universal humanism pulsating deep within different cultures. People of religion who want to contribute to world peace must undertake the proud mission of enlightening others about this deeper humanism. This is the challenge leaders in the twenty-first century must face.

Ikeda: I have always acted in the belief that enlightening others about humanism is the humane and social mission of the religious. With whatever strength is at my command, I have consistently undertaken the task of illuminating the humanistic philosophy and spirit deep within various cultures. The dialogues I have published with thinkers from all over the world, and the speeches I have delivered at Harvard University and many other institutes of higher education, are part of my work to this end.

The future fate of our planet depends in large measure on the extent to which we can strengthen and expand human abilities to engage in dialogue. If, as the Spanish philosopher Ortega y Gasset said, violence is the Magna Carta of barbarism, dialogue can be called the Magna Carta of civilization. We must establish the Magna Carta of civilization in the twenty-first century by pursuing the course that encourages dialogue throughout the world.

TEN

New Paths for Education

_____

Becoming a citizen of the world

Ikeda: You are an intrepid, tireless fieldworker who has travelled extensively in Europe, the Middle East and India performing highly valuable cultural-anthropological investigations.

Yalman: Fieldwork is the life of a cultural anthropologist. I believe a teacher must be willing to travel any distance in the search for truth.

Ikeda: Yes, that is true. What kind of education enabled you to become a global citizen with knowledge encompassing all humanity?

Yalman: Four things have had an influence on me. First, the gentle, traditional culture of Ottoman humanism. I learned this at the feet of my grandfather, who was a Sufi poet and a brilliant Islamic calligrapher. Second, British and American scholarly and political writings – my uncle, a celebrated editor of a major liberal newspaper in Turkey, taught me the critical elements of political liberty in public life in the English and American traditions. These influenced me profoundly, especially in my years at Cambridge University. While there, I became deeply interested in French and German philosophy. Continental philosophy from Hegel to Sartre and Lévi-Strauss is the third element in my intellectual development.

Perhaps most important of all is the fourth element – my deep involvement in the civilization of the Indian subcontinent. During fieldwork in Sri Lanka, I learned a great deal about Buddhist enlightenment. My work in India opened my eyes to the extraordinary intellectual riches still in evidence in South Asia, in the forms of Hinduism, Jainism, Sikhism, South Asian Islam and others. In addition, work in Iran, Iraq and Turkey as well as more general Islamic traditions contributed to my development. I feel that I am the product of the intellectual currents coming from all four sources. I feel at home in both Eastern and Western traditions.

Ikeda: That is a wonderful thing. Contact with diverse cultural environments engenders great wisdom. The opportunity for such contacts, made possible by the ancient Silk Road connecting East and West, produced numerous outstanding figures. Because of their activities, many Buddhist scriptures, including the Lotus Sutra, were translated and transmitted to China, the Korean Peninsula and Japan. The Arab world of the Middle Ages – which passed on the heritage of India, Classical Greece and Rome to Renaissance Italy – is another example of diverse cultural influences. The United States, a virtual melting pot of all kinds of cultural traditions, has made great contributions to the advance of science and culture. Istanbul, where you grew up, symbolizes the blending of East and West. All these instances prove that promoting attitudes of openness to the world is the best way to cultivate world citizens.

What influence does Japan exert?

Yalman: As a modern person, I have been trying to learn as much as possible about Japanese intellectual traditions. Without doubt, Japan is an important model for all non-Western societies.

120

Ikeda: It is very generous of you to say so. In this wonderful course of development, you have encountered many cultures and met many different kinds of people.

Yalman: Yes, I have. I sincerely consider myself very fortunate to have received a comprehensively rich and varied education. Although I was brought up in Turkish schools, I was taught French and German early in life. Later, at Cambridge, I met many wonderful, open-minded people who were very interested in wisdom and the life of the intellect. I am happy to have spent so much time in fieldwork and research activities in Asia. I believe that, together with dialogue, education is the basis of world peace.

As a long-standing advocate of the importance of examining good educational methods in both the East and the West, I am very impressed that Soka University of America is stimulating a fresh impetus in humanistic education. As an educational institution with a totally new kind of mission, it will reveal whether we can put into practice our ideas about human brotherhood, peace and the uses of history and science. I wish Soka University great success in this endeavour.

Education above all

Ikeda: Soka University of America and Soka University in Japan are realizations of the dreams of Tsunesaburo Makiguchi and Josei Toda. The primary aim of both is to educate popular leaders who can contribute to world peace and the happiness of humanity.

All the world leaders with whom I have spoken agree that education is absolutely fundamental to human happiness, social prosperity and world peace. In the search for social development and reform, concentrating exclusively on the political and economic dimensions is bound to lead to an impasse, as indeed it has already done. All serious thinkers have come to the conclusion that, though it may seem indirect, education is the surest way.

Yalman: I agree. Education is the most important issue facing society. We ought to encourage education that promotes awareness of the ways of life of other peoples. Here I think a great task falls upon anthropologists, whose entire purpose is to elucidate apparently exotic lifestyles.

Ikeda: In connection with education, Arnold J. Toynbee warned, 'A human being can be manipulated insofar as he can be dehumanized.'[1] Bellicose education, the supreme example of his meaning, causes unhappiness and suffering and throws society into turmoil. Having grown up in a time buffeted by the winds of war, I know this from personal experience. In Japan, when the militarist pall enveloped all of society, educating for the exclusive purpose of serving the state cost many young lives, including those of many friends and acquaintances, as well as my own eldest brother.

Yalman: Turkey was not dragged into the Second World War. Nonetheless, as a person of your generation, I sympathize with your experiences of the folly and misery of war. It is a matter of deep sadness and disappointment to observe that the political leaders of great countries like the United States, Britain, France and numerous others have not learned the lessons of two world wars that took untold numbers of precious lives.

In addition to these world wars, many other wars must weigh on our minds. Two of the most unnecessary were the wars in Vietnam and Algeria. Since the arrival in the region of the Western powers, the countries of the Middle East have also had no respite. Many of these conflicts have been initiated in the name of national interests for the narrow personal gains of small coteries in control of state military apparatuses. Even President Eisenhower was aware of their power and cautioned against the dangers of the military-industrial complex.

Ikeda: We must remember that many lives have been lost for the sake of national interests or various other advantages and we must find ways to transmit awareness of this tragedy to coming generations.

During the Second World War, Soka Gakkai presidents Makiguchi and Toda opposed war-oriented education and struggled to promote humane behaviour. For their efforts, they were sent to prison. Mr Makiguchi died there; Mr Toda was released after years of imprisonment. Their spirit and strength, even in the face of oppression, was the starting point of all Soka Gakkai activities for peace, culture and education. Religious faith supports the battle for human rights. Both Mr Makiguchi and Mr Toda believed that religion without educational backing often becomes self-righteous, complacent, self-absorbed and isolated from society. The connection between education and religion must become a major focal point of the twenty-first century.

A sense of communal responsibility

Yalman: Though their traditions differ, instead of dwelling on each other's failings, religions ought to celebrate each other's merits. I am dismayed by the extraordinary ignorance people display about each other. Neither Western ignorance about Eastern religions nor Eastern ignorance about Western religions is acceptable. The ignorance is very entrenched and can only be dispelled through better education and the kind of work you do. Josei Toda and Tsunesaburo Makiguchi were entirely correct to think the problem of education is central to the future of humankind. Our task is to implement their philosophies. That is why we anthropologists must encourage education that cultivates caring for others. The sense of empathy is the foundation of our humanism.

Ikeda: Mention of education and empathy calls to mind Visva-Bharati University founded by the Indian poet Rabindranath

Tagore in 1901 in a beautiful, natural setting at Santiniketan. Taking as a school motto 'All the world living in a single nest', Tagore wanted to create a place where different ethnic groups and cultures could assemble. He invited scholars and intellectuals from all over the world to come to stimulate young minds. Many students from other countries gathered there.

Not long ago, we welcomed a group from the university and discussed working together to carry on the ideal of the united human spirit. Universally, education propagating correct values and views of the world will provide hope for the peace and prosperity of humanity.

Your belief that anthropologists must open the minds of humanity to others impresses me deeply. All other fields of learning must adopt the same attitude.

Yalman: Quite true. Many of the problems and tragedies of the world today arise because people immersed in their daily lives in one civilization fail to respect the ways of life of other civilizations. To appreciate the rich traditions of humanity one must open oneself up as much as possible to other languages, philosophies and experiences and learn from the merits of other people how to enrich our own community. I have tried to do this with my children, who have now all finished university. Some of them have become academics and, to my great pleasure, all speak several languages.

Ikeda: Because of the importance of linguistic studies, the Soka high schools emphasize languages – especially English – in order to cultivate international awareness from an early age. Young people bear the responsibility for the future; international awareness is the foundation on which they must build a world of symbiosis and coexistence.

Evaluating the past

Yalman: History is a key subject because it is the area where both good and evil reside. In the preparation of historical works, one can demonize enemies. On the other hand, an effective and intelligent handling of history can make past tragedies less negative and may lead to their reconsideration and re-evaluation. For instance, accomplished modern historians have now begun to question the necessity of the First World War and try to determine who created the conditions leading to it.

Ikeda: Without strict verification of history, human beings are liable to repeat past mistakes. Even the tremendous scars left by the First World War did not prevent the outbreak of the Second World War. It is crucial that we should learn lessons from this historical fact.

This is true in cases other than those of war. Barren ideological conflicts and radical thought brought on many of the tragedies of the twentieth century. No one can confidently predict that such tragedies will not recur in the twenty-first century. Ten years ago, Mikhail S. Gorbachev, who helped bring the Cold War to a conclusion, said he wanted a thorough-going inquiry into history to be the core of the dialogue we were initiating at the time. This is why we called the book recording our dialogue *Moral Lessons of the Twentieth Century*.

Yalman: Concentrating on recent, often insufficiently studied, history is vital. We must question the nuclear bombs dropped on Japan, the bombing of Dresden and the horrors visited upon the Jews by the Germans. The terrible atrocities performed by all groups in the world wars of the twentieth century must be reconsidered and re-examined. Though assigning guilt is difficult, history is a very critical area to think about.

It is the historians' responsibility to show that no one has clean hands. To my mind, their work must include the great suffering that, during the First World War, befell the Armenian people and the Turkish and Kurdish populations who had

125

previously shared their lives and cultures in a neighbourly, generally affable, way. All war is terrible, but civil war of this kind inflicts the most intimate of horrors.

Ikeda: We must both look back in history and forward towards possible future developments. The first courageous step towards peace is accurate and unflinching verification of the inhuman acts of one's own nation, be they invasion or war.

Yalman: In the last chapter of his *The Savage Mind*, Claude Lévi-Strauss wrote that history and mythology are very closely related and that history has a mythological element. Everything depends on how we reconstruct the past for our own purposes. In a sense, then, history plays a role very similar to that of religion and therefore must be handled with great care, gravity and intelligence.

Education, religion and common human truths

Ikeda: In both recording history now and investigating the history of the past, everything depends on the nature of the person handling the material. And this is why education, which nurtures the handlers of history, is of the utmost importance. As I have already said, I lay great emphasis on the relation between education and religion. Education brings life to flower and illuminates the soul. It enables people to find a foothold for activity as part of society and to manifest their abilities. For its part, religion enriches human nature and inspires passion for improvement. Empathy born of these processes makes it impossible to overlook others' unhappiness and generates the strength to save others. When religion and education influence each other in the best sense, they stabilize society and guide it towards peace and happiness.

Yalman: For years, I have observed how you and the members of Soka Gakkai accept the challenge of this difficult task. I am deeply moved by the way Soka Gakkai members open themselves to society and, taking faith as their starting point, strive to live as good individuals.

Ikeda: In the United States and many other parts of the world, Soka Gakkai members conduct pacific, cultural and educational activities with the aim of being good citizens who create society-enriching values. Their way of life derives from Mahayana teachings about the nature of the bodhisattva.

One aspect of Buddhism stresses the mundane, spiritual realm, not affected by the constantly changing world of ordinary experience. At the same time, however, it emphasizes participating in the ordinary world by carrying out value-creating actions there. Instead of existing in isolation from its ceaseless change, the bodhisattva plunges directly into society to establish a firm footing for vigorous social activity. This is the way of living Nichiren taught and demonstrated.

Yalman: Religions bound up in their own dogmas close their minds. They are soon overcome by fanatics who reject the others' worlds. They thus lose contact with the whole of humanity to such an extent that they become incapable of harmonizing, stabilizing and improving society. The best way for religions to make their teachings known, understood and accepted throughout the world is to avoid self-centred, arrogant fanaticism.

There are many truths before us. Only acts of peace will fertilize creative cultural exchanges. Of course, such activities must always be founded on a noble spirit. Social conformity is not the issue. We must try to evoke common human truths deep within traditional religions so that, in time, we can develop them into universal human wisdom. If handled in a spirit of generosity, traditional teachings can be revived to become a driving force for transcending difficult times, overcoming cultural differences and creating a sympathetic human world.

Ikeda: Such is the goal of our Soka Gakkai inter-civilization and inter-religion dialogues. We want people to put their shared humanity ahead of religious affiliation – Buddhist, Muslim or Christian. When, as a result of dialogue, friendship emerges from awareness of our shared humanity, we will come to see each other's strengths and weaknesses clearly and will want to learn from each other. Instead of thinking about each other as members of some specific religious organization, we will know each other's faces and call each other by our names. When we relate at this level, true inter-civilization and inter-religion dialogue results.

Encounters that impel history

Yalman: Today we can make daily contacts over vast distances all around the world. I can speak from Cambridge to my friends in Tokyo instantly. These fairly recent technological developments are certain to progress further. However, since increased contacts can provoke unsuspected schisms, our communications must take the form of more attentive and meaningful dialogue.

Ikeda: Very true. As globalization proceeds, conflicts and abuses turn people's minds inward, resulting in significant divisions and social friction. For this reason, we have an unprecedented need for mutual understanding, founded on amity and solidarity, and the willingness to transcend ideologies to cope with the global problem.

I have discussed critical matters with experts in many fields from all over the world. The differences of opinion revealed in dialogue make possible new discoveries for both participants. I am resolved to go on pursuing the course of education and dialogue to the maximum.

Yalman: You have already made great contributions. Your dialogues on civilization and religion are a bridge uniting the peoples of the world. By providing forums where intelligent discussions on momentous topics can take place you perform a service of great value to all mankind.

Ikeda: You give me too much credit. I am deeply grateful for the opportunity to have participated in this dialogue, which has taught me much about anthropological and Islamic views. As Arnold J. Toynbee pointed out, human history is no simple cycle. It is capable of unexpected developments. He believed chance encounters between individuals to be the area in which we can expect to find fluid patterns in human affairs. Such encounters lead to true innovation. I believe our mission is the endless pursuit of dialogue and the kind of creative encounters that change history.

APPENDIX 1

The Kemalist Revolution: A Model

A speech delivered by Daisaku Ikeda at Ankara University, Turkey, 24 June 1992

I am deeply grateful to receive an honorary doctorate from Ankara University, an academic institution of long and distinguished tradition, founded by the first president of the Republic of Turkey and 'father of the Turks', Mustafa Kemal Atatürk. It is also an honour to have been invited to speak today, and I would like to thank the university rector, Dr Necdet Serin, the members of the university and the many distinguished guests who have gathered here.

A Japanese scholar who was very knowledgeable about Turkey once referred to it as 'distant, yet close'. The two countries are separated by a vast geographical distance, one being located by the Mediterranean sea and the other off the eastern shore of the Eurasian continent. Yet, surprisingly, there are cultural and ethnic affinities between the two. Three months ago, I met Professor Nur Yalman, an eminent Turkish cultural anthropologist currently teaching at Harvard University. He reminded me of several parallels between our homelands. First there is evidence dating far back into pre-history that points to similar racial origins for Japanese and Turks in Central Asia. Also, our countries were situated at either end of the Silk Road, which was for centuries a medium of cultural and commercial exchange between different peoples. Perhaps for this reason, there are some unexpected similarities in the languages, customs and traditions of Turkey and Japan even today. In Professor Yalman's words, we are 'natural allies'.

The Turkish people place a great deal of importance on friendship. Perhaps that is best symbolized by the word for comradeship, *arkadaçlik*, but fidelity and courage are also central to their value system. A vibrant brand of universalism and humanism is very apparent in Turkey. That spirit is crystallized in two lines written by the poet Yunus Emre, whose words resound with force and clarity across seven centuries:

> I am not here on earth for strife,
> Love is the mission of my life.[1]

The world faces an extraordinary drama of change in the closing years of the twentieth century. The establishment of a new and peaceful international order will mean replacing the hard power of economic, military and political instruments with new tools of soft power such as systems, laws, information and peaceful negotiation.

In his lecture at Soka University in 1990, Rector Serin pointed out that we are seeing the transition from an age of absolute and monolithic authority and ideology to an age in which decisions are made through the collective wisdom of the people. I believe that the way to peace lies in extending and strengthening the international system already in place, albeit in nascent and imperfect form – the core of which is the United Nations. To build a new international order based on peace, we must encourage strong support from the public around the world. Furthermore, we need a spiritual foundation, or zeitgeist, that will let the new system function well. Our organization, Soka Gakkai International, in its capacity as an NGO (non-governmental organization), is trying to do its part by consistently supporting the objectives of the United Nations.

The themes of Kemalism

I would now like to talk about some of the underlying themes of Kemalism, which can be considered the national philosophy of modern Turkey. Coined after Kemal Atatürk, who developed its principal concepts as a base for his sweeping reforms, the essence of Kemalism is much more than a type of Westernization. It represents, rather, a remarkable series of choices coming out of Turkey's long and extraordinarily rich historical experience as a witness to the rise and fall of many cultures and civilizations. Kemalism is the product of a land that is at a central crossroads of our globe. The great city known to the world at different times as Byzantium, Constantinople and Istanbul is a fitting symbol of this meeting of East and West.

The six principles of Kemalism are: republicanism, nationalism, populism, statism, secularism and reformism. They constitute a framework that is filled with and held firm by openness of spirit and striving toward the universal. Kemal Atatürk's overriding desire and goal was to awaken the Turkish people to their potential in the modern world. As his motto 'make new friends, but treasure old ones' suggests, he successfully avoided the pitfalls of parochial nationalism in seeking to open his nation and his people to the world, and in so doing he proclaimed the universal nature of his vision.

Both Kemal Atatürk as a man and Kemalism as a set of principles demonstrate a coherent and developed sense of balance and proportion, a trait that has proved to be highly effective. Atatürk the valiant reformer was given at times to explosive passions, but his actions were always governed by a will of steel and a strong sense of moderation. The annals of world history would have to be searched exhaustively to find another individual who could remain as self-possessed and in control through the upheaval that accompanied such a momentous attempt at reform as Turkey's. By its massive scope, depth and thoroughness, it compared, in the words of Arnold Toynbee, to 'the Renaissance, the Reformation, the secularist, scientific [revolution] . . . the French Revolution, and the Industrial Revolution . . . telescoped into a single lifetime . . .'[2] And while Atatürk was bringing new life to his country, his contemporaries Hitler, Mussolini and Stalin gave in to the dark temptation of domination and brought instead untold suffering as they tumbled to destruction.

Atatürk was intensely conscious of the demonic nature of power, particularly because the scale and scope of his own were so great. During the last years of his life, understanding the pitfalls of so much concentrated authority, he tried to abolish the one-party system and deliberately create an opposition. The effort proved premature, but the move to voluntarily relinquish absolute power was heroic and virtually unique in modern history.

Atatürk was also able to balance the merits of each situation, even if he seemed to contradict himself. For example, the last years of the Ottoman Empire left him with bitter memories, and he was extremely wary of foreign investment or interference in Turkish affairs, to the extent that to some he seemed xenophobic. Yet he welcomed teachers and instructors from other countries. His enlightened approach to education, to name only one area, bore all the hallmarks of his moderation and restraint – certainly not passionate anti-foreignism. He also had the foresight to focus on long-term developments and to steer clear, for example, of any pan-Turkish ambitions. Having secured the borders and territory of the new-born state, he never used military force against any of his neighbours.

We who live in this day and age urgently need the qualities of character that Atatürk had. The concerns of people in the contemporary world increasingly are transnational and global, and they demand moderation and restraint. We can no longer afford to let dogmatic or parochial views inform our actions; we must develop the ability to see ourselves objectively with respect to the rest of the world. Only those with far-sighted open-mindedness can aspire to globalism. The ability to strike a balance between one's own interests and those of other nations – or, at a deeper level, between the individual and the universal

– is the mark of the world citizen. In the long run, these are the qualities that must become the spiritual foundation for the rules and structures of a just international order.

İsmet İnönü succeeded Atatürk as president of Turkey. During his tenure, and in accordance with the will of his predecessor, Turkey established a multi-party system and carried out a democratic transfer of power. Arnold Toynbee celebrated this event as 'a notable triumph for a sense of fair play and moderation in politics,'[3] the essential components of the open spirit and universalist thrust of Kemalism.

On the people's side

Like Atatürk himself, Kemalism stands for the well-being of the people. A philosophy that is truly universal does not hover in some abstract limbo; it penetrates the hearts, souls and lives of the people. Transmitted from heart to heart, it crosses borders to unify the world. Humanity itself is the soil from which universality springs.

Now and then I try to express my feelings in poetry. Let me quote one part of a verse I wrote to celebrate ordinary, common people:

> People!
> you alone are reality
> outside of you there is no real world
>
> Science without you is cold-hearted
> philosophy without you is barren
> art without you is empty
> religion without you is merciless[4]

My attempt at poetry is paltry compared with the moving, famous speech that Atatürk delivered before the National Assembly in August 1926. In that speech, he proclaimed, 'Every great movement must find its source in the depths of a people's soul, the original spring of all strengths and greatness. Failing this, all is ruin and dust.'

The unfailing confidence of his words grew, no doubt, from his unparalleled record of achievement as a leader deeply engaged with and committed to the people. Whether in battle, or in the less lethal arenas of politics and education, he always fought alongside his countrymen, sharing their suffering and joys and urging them to greater awareness and pride as Turks. Through his brave and dedicated efforts, he gave new courage to a country exhausted and despondent from war. He revolutionized the consciousness of a nation, directing popular energy towards the construction of a new Turkey. In doing this, he rescued his nation from a crisis that threatened its very existence.

The transformation Atatürk led in his country is possible in other countries, as well. When it happens, and when people of all countries feel the same healthy pride in their identity, they will emerge as world citizens. This outlook does not submerge ethnic distinctions; rather, it enhances the unique qualities of each society. People who have been awakened to their global responsibilities will join hands in universal solidarity, each in their own way contributing their special assets.

Education is the precondition for spiritual unification, and it was a priority under Atatürk. Insofar as education was one of its major pillars, the Kemalist revolution was not radical, though on the surface it might have appeared to be. That it took, in fact, a gradualist approach may have been the factor that ensured the success of the revolution.

The process of sublimation that leads to a wider, more universal perception of the world operates through the interaction and mutual stimulation of peoples and cultures, namely, through education. I use this term in the broadest sense, including dialogue as a mode of learning. The words of Professor Yalman remind us that education is the most direct and certain path to the universal and, hence, to world peace. It is certainly education that lets us transcend different backgrounds and discover commonalities. It enables us to think on a higher plane – that is, as a human being; to free ourselves from thinking that is based solely on membership of a particular faction or school.

136

The Kemalist revolution was a cultural transformation of great scope and depth, but nowhere was it more successful than in the area of educational reform. Atatürk used education to create a 'new Turkey' and a 'new Turkish people'. Among all his achievements, this was accomplished with an earthy practicality and personal engagement that were noble, idealistic and very effective. I have an image of the first president, blackboard and chalk in hand, travelling to all corners of the new republic to teach his countrymen the romanized Turkish alphabet that he himself had devised.

Citizens of the nation, citizens of the world

Behind all he achieved at the national level is Atatürk's view of civilization. He saw it in terms of its universal values. In 1921, speaking of the need to eliminate deep-rooted enmity between ethnic groups, Atatürk stated: 'It is not by military victories that we shall do this, but only by reaching for everything that modern knowledge and civilization demand, and by actually attaining the cultural level realized by all civilized peoples.'[5]

Atatürk believed in the ideal of cultural progress to instil global values. It was the force that would enable the Turkish people to become good citizens of their nation, and thereby to become good citizens of the world. His ideas predate the eclipse of the Europe-centred positivist view of history, perhaps best articulated in Oswald Spengler's *The Decline of the West* (1923). While Spengler saw civilization as moving along an inevitable, linear path, our experience of history has provided ample proof that civilization moves in ways that are not simple, linear or inevitable. Furthermore, the influence of Western values has been undermined by new theories in anthropology developed in this century. The paradigm of cultural relativism, which rejects hierarchical evaluation of cultures and civilizations, has been particularly influential.

Atatürk, however, remained firmly convinced that the process of cultural enhancement would enable the Turkish people to realize higher, global values as world citizens. In other words, his thinking is characterized by his aspiration toward the universal. With fresh ideas and an open heart, he sought a new place in history for his beloved homeland.

Many students of Atatürk's life share my belief that his policies were guided not simply by hypothetical ideals but by a specific historical model. If any, it is probably the French Revolution, which Atatürk studied intensely during his youth. Let us say, then, that France and the French people of that time provided the model for Turkey's new constitution and its educational system. The twentieth-century French philosopher Simone Weil described the universal appeal of revolutionary France:

> The Revolution melted all the peoples subject to the French Crown into one single mass . . . by their enthusiasm for national sovereignty. Those who had been Frenchmen by force, became so by free consent; many of those who were not French wanted to become so.[6]

Replace 'France' with 'Turkey' in this passage, and we have an idea of Atatürk's vision of a new Turkish people.

In recent years, Turkey has become the focus of growing attention for its role as a meeting place of Eastern and Western civilizations. This stems from more than economic interests or religious and ethnic ties with other countries. Rather, it indicates the universal appeal of the enlightened philosophy of Kemalism. It is very likely that the spirit of the Turkish national motto, 'Peace at Home, Peace Abroad' will inspire other countries as they deal with the volatile international context of our times. I can envision an enchanting, peaceful future when many peoples, including the Japanese, will be able to travel a new Silk Road of cultural exchange and mutual understanding. This will be a channel for individuals to share and deepen their appreciation of the universal values of human dignity, harmony with nature and responsibility to future generations. Those values will equip us with the means to resolve the complex global problems before us. I, too, pledge to do my utmost to help achieve this milestone in the quest for world peace.

I will conclude with an expression of hope and resolve by Yunus Emre that in two lines articulates my feelings better than I could ever do:

> The world to me is sustenance,
> Its peoples and my own are one.[7]

APPENDIX 2

Terror and Cultural Diversity in Times of Adversity

A speech delivered by Nur Yalman at the forum of the Transnational Foundation for Peace and Future Research, Cambridge, 23 February 2002.

The problem of cultural paranoia

My topic today is Terrorism and Cultural Diversity. The tragic events of September 11 are still reverberating around the world. I am sure that the question of the role of cultural diversity in providing the breeding ground for 'terror' is on many people's minds. Does 'terror' arise from cultural distance? Is it the 'foreigners', those people we do not understand, who are the 'troublemakers'? To be anxious about strangers in our midst is a natural reaction. In times of fear and panic, the 'aliens', the 'foreigners' become suspect. We must be very careful to distinguish between realistic threats to security from those paranoid reactions against all foreigners. The very great danger in times of crisis is the focusing of anxiety and anger on outsiders. This leads to 'ethnic profiling', or 'stereotyping', and then, as a direct result of this, the 'scapegoating' of innocents. Such times are also very convenient for unscrupulous politicians to manipulate the public mood for their advantage.

I do not wish to minimize the scale of the disaster that struck New York and Washington. It is, however, also true that in the panic that ensued, the major constitutional safeguards for individual liberties were swept aside in a stampede for national security in America. The Patriot Act has given the US president very wide discretionary powers. 'Foreigners' can now be arrested, tried with secret evidence in secret trials and they can be sentenced to death in the US. This can be done all the more easily in an American military base like Guantánamo, which is outside the jurisdiction of US courts. Hence the delicate diplomatic status of the Taliban and al-Qaeda prisoners held there. This situation is no different from the notorious 'disappearances' of persons in Chile, Argentina and elsewhere. Fortunately, there has been serious opposition to these policies: it is reported that the administration, under pressure from its European allies, has finally decided to change its position on the status of these prisoners. The International Geneva Convention will now be applied to them (*New York Times*, 23 February 2002).

We have seen the tragic consequences of these kinds of reactions in our recent history. The burning of the Reichstag in Germany gave the Nazis the excuse to attack those elements they regarded as alien to German society. The results were disastrous. There are similar histories associated with the ordeal of Koreans during the Tokyo earthquake in Japan at the end of the First World War, but it must be admitted that no society is totally immune to these profound troubles, which represent a combination of psychological, anthropological and political anxieties.

The personal tragedies associated with the McCarthy era in the US have not been forgotten. Large numbers of brilliant people were smeared with the broad brush of Communism. They were accused, harassed and forced to escape their country.

I had numerous friends in Cambridge, England, who had found refuge in the brilliant intellectual circles of a great university, which had provided a home for these unfortunate Americans. One of the most outstanding of these people was Moses Finley, the great classicist. He was originally Mr Finkelstein, a Jew from New York. He refused the 'loyalty oath' that was demanded by his university. Accused as a 'commie', he left for England in 1956. He was so much appreciated in England that he rose to become the master of Jesus College in Cambridge and was knighted by the Queen – he ended his stellar career as Sir Moses Finley. So, in times of crisis, cultural and ethnic categories and the accusations they may lead to may become highly dangerous weapons for the body politic.

Focus on 'scapegoats'

The unfolding of the human disasters in the heart of Europe during the ethnic conflict in the Balkans a few years ago, began with simple stereotypes and then escalated into political murder as cathartic human sacrifice. There was the stereotype of the 'enemy' for the Serbs; the 'enemy' was defined as the 'Muslims' and dehumanized. The use of the media (especially television) in categorizing, labelling and stereotyping the 'target' populations was crucial in this respect.

The process outlined above can be readily adapted to different situations. The *New Yorker* (15 March 1993, p.4) ran a Comment entitled 'Quiet Voices from the Balkans'. It reported on the visit to New York of the editor of *Vreme* ('the only independent magazine still publishing in Belgrade'), Vasic, and a professor of law from Sarajevo, Pajic. This is what Vasic was reportedly saying:

> Both stations began to traffic in stereotypes ... On Belgrade TV, the Croats became *Ustashas*. On Zagreb TV, all Serbs were *Chetniks*. These are terms from the Second World War that today are ethnic insults. And then both stations began to play with the notion that Muslims are unreliable dangerous fundamentalists.

You could just watch these stations and know that something really big was rolling behind. [What was rolling behind . . . was war.] . . . It is very easy . . . First you create fear, then distrust, then panic. Then all you have to do is come every night and distribute submachine guns in every village, and you are ready.

These comments of Vasic were evidently not to the liking of the American correspondent for Belgrade government television. The *New Yorker* ends the Comment: 'That detail made it especially chilling, somehow, when she glared at Mr Vasic, her fellow Serbian journalist and spat "Traitor!"' Note the pattern – frustration, the focusing of anger, scapegoats, sacrificial violence. And behind all this generating, manipulating and directing the passions – political agents calculating their moves with the care and attention of chess masters.

It is thus that all the daily frustrations of the unfortunate masses in the streets can be mobilized to attack those institutions which are held to be responsible for their sorry state of affairs. Liberal institutions of government, the more clear-headed newspapers, those who might claim that the 'hated' populations have some 'constitutional rights' – all these 'soft' nationalists can then be ridiculed or worse, attacked and frightened. Step by inexorable step, one moves towards a dismantling of 'constitutional liberal' safeguards, until the levers of power are in the grasp of the most unscrupulous of political elements. This is, in outline, what had happened, fortunately for a short period, in Sri Lanka. (S.J. Tambiah, *Buddhism Betrayed? Religion, Politics and Violence in Sri Lanka* (Chicago: University of Chicago Press, 1992)). There are hopeful signs today that we may see the end of that disastrous conflict, which has cost almost 100,000 lives among the Sinhalese and Tamils.

We have been much more fortunate in the case of India. The extraordinary complexity of languages, traditions, castes and ethnicities have been accommodated by a reasonable constitution and representative institutions so that the many potential dangers have been avoided. The danger of conflict, however, is always in the wings. We have all heard how the whole of India used to come to a stop when the great epics of

144

the *Mahābhārata* and the *Rāmāyana* were being aired on national TV some years ago. But there evidently was also an underlying message – a targeting going on – towards perceived 'alien' elements.

This process has the psychological advantage of focusing frustration on people perceived as 'outsiders', 'foreigners', 'immigrants' – even if they have lived in the country for centuries. So one can pretend, for example, that Muslims – all 130 million of them who are as local as can be imagined – do not really belong to India. They came too late – only 1,000 years ago – they are still not Hindus, and it is time for them to leave. (See also, Susanne H. Rudolph and Lloyd R. Rudolph, 'Modern Hate', in *The New Republic*, 22 March 1993, pp.24–9).

The Calais incident

Some years ago, the *New York Times* (30 October 1992) reported on a remarkable incident in Calais, north France. A rumour had suddenly swept through the town that a dark-skinned fellow, a stranger, had been kidnapping, raping, torturing and killing some children from one of the local schools for some infernal purpose. As the rumour spread, anxious parents converged on the school to save their children. The principal was called out to meet the parents. He denied that any such incident had taken place at his school. No one believed him. The matter got onto nationwide TV in France. A swarthy ex-drug addict, part-Algerian, whose French mother lived in Calais, was 'discovered'. He was accused of committing the heinous crimes. He barely escaped with his life. After considerable commotion, it was clearly established that no child was missing, no murder had taken place and that there was no basis at all for the panic. The 'Algerian' could not be accused of any tangible misdeed. The townspeople remained unsure: some dark act had to have taken place – which was being denied by the authorities as usual. Eventually, the 'Algerian' escaped to the safety of Paris. Calais simmered down. By way of explanation, the *New York*

Times suggested that unemployment and frustration with the economic situation had been particularly high in this neglected north-eastern corner of France.

There are obviously many ways of approaching the complex subject of 'ethnic labelling' and 'scapegoats'. However, the question of political manipulation, the political psychology of crowd-hysteria, of 'targeting' and the focusing of mass frustration is evident. The cases mentioned above may provide some basis for further thoughts on the subject. This is something on which there is much to be said from an anthropological perspective.

The experience of Islam and India

While there is always the danger of 'categories' being utilized for political mischief, we are also well aware of the different experiences of civilizations on the question of diversity. I would argue that both in the Islamic empires and in India – in other words a vast area of the ancient world – the very complexity of the ethnic background of the populations was so great that difference became an everyday matter. The acceptance of difference as a matter of course in one's life rendered human relations more tolerant. It was part of the fabric of life. You could speak one language at home, another one in the school, a third one with your neighbours and a fourth one in the market. No one would be surprised at that anywhere in India or, to a lesser extent, in Western Asia. While the language issue might not have given rise to such a rich variety, the Islamic societies managed the human relations between the different elements without resorting to caste divisions, as in the case of the Indian subcontinent.

So cultural diversity need not lead to trouble and division. It can increase the cultural richness and creativity of a society. It does however need good and effective administration. The bloody European experience of the nineteenth century, with nationalist ideologies and extensive ethnic cleansing on the

146

continent, must make us wary of lurking totalitarian attitudes in diversified societies.

Allow me to give you some sense of the complexities involved.

On diversity in West Asia

It was Mansur, the second Abbasid caliph (754–75) who built the city of Baghdad on the banks of the Tigris, near the ruins of the old Sassanid capital of Ctesiphon. The geographer Ya'qubi describes the idea:

> This island between the Tigris in the East and the Euphrates in the West is a market place for the world. All the ships that come up the Tigris from Wāsit, Basra, Ubulla, Ahwāz, Fars, Umān, Yamāma, Bahrain and beyond will go up and anchor here; wares brought on ships down the Tigris from Mosul, Diyār-Rabī'a, Adharbaijān and Armenia, and along the Euphrates from Diyār-Mudar, Raqqa, Syria and the border marshes, Egypt and North Africa will be brought and unloaded here. It will be the highway for the people of the Jabal, Isfāhān and the districts of Khurāsān ... It will surely be the most flourishing city in the world. (Bernard Lewis, *The Arabs in History* (Oxford: Oxford University Press, 1954), p.82)

So, Baghdad was to be a great trading centre. The civilization of the early Islamic empire fulfilled those hopes. Historians report that

> ... Muslim merchants [leaving the Gulf ports] travelled to India, Ceylon, the East Indies and China, bringing silks, spices, aromatics, woods, tin and other commodities ... Alternative routes to India and China ran overland through Central Asia. The goods brought from China included silk, crockery, paper, ink, peacocks, horses, saddles, felt, cinnamon, rhubarb; from the Byzantine Empire ... gold and silver utensils, gold coins, drugs, brocades, slave girls, trinkets, locks, hydraulic engineers, agronomes, marble workers and eunuchs; from India ... tigers, panthers, elephants, panther skins, rubies, white sandalwood, ebony and coconuts.

Muslim navigators were quite at home in eastern seas, where Arab traders were established in China as early as the eighth century.

There was also extensive trade between the Islamic empire and the Baltic via the Caspian, the Black Sea and Russia. 'With Africa too, the Arabs carried on an extensive overland trade.' The Jews served as a link with Europe. The early ninth-century geographer, Ibn Khurradadhbeh, tells of Jewish merchants from the south of France:

> ... who speak Arabic, Persian, Greek, Frankish, Spanish, and Slavonic. They travel from west to east and from east to west, by land and by sea. From the west they bring eunuchs, slave-girls, boys, brocade, castor-skins, marten and other furs and swords ... they sail on the eastern (Red) Sea from Qulzum to Al-Jār and Jedda, and onward to Sind, India and China. From China they bring back musk, aloes, camphor, cinnamon, and other products ... Some sail with their goods to Constantinople, and sell them to the Greeks, and some take them to the king of Franks and sell them there.

In other words, a 'common market' without boundaries and with considerable mobility was evidently a characteristic of the brilliant period of the early Islamic empire. The historian again: 'We hear of banks with a head office in Baghdad and branches in the other cities of the Empire and of an elaborate system of cheques, letters of credit, etc., so developed that it was possible to draw a cheque in Baghdad and cash it in Morocco'(Lewis, *The Arabs in History*).

It was this coherence of the Islamic lands within their immense diversity that the Ottoman Empire had tried to preserve against the predatory attacks from the West. It is astonishing also that they were relatively successful in doing so until 1918, the end of the First World War.

The reason it is worth mentioning these matters is two-fold: first, the idea of a 'common market' among Muslim countries at least, is as old as Islam, and second, a sense of security and easy personal relations with full freedom of movement was the norm until very recent times. After all, it was not at all surprising for the intrepid and indefatigable traveller Ibn Batuta to go from Fez and Meknes in Morocco all the way to Cairo, Anatolia, Crimea, Baghdad, Delhi and the Maldives and to be received as a learned *alim* (professor) in the royal courts of all those places. He even found the time and energy to make a trip to West Africa after his return to Fez.

A more controversial recent example may be the sorry adventure of Osama bin Laden and his al-Qaeda Arabs in Afghanistan. How is it that these Arabs, who did not speak a word of the local Pashto language were somehow accepted and given a respectable welcome in a most unlikely context? There is a story to be told here. We have not yet heard the anthropological side of it.

Terror, diversity? Freedom fighters?

Now what about 'terror'? Does cultural diversity as such provide the fertile ground for acts of terror? I mentioned above in connection with the Balkans or Sri Lanka how trouble ensues when matters are allowed to get out of hand. But this is no different than relations within a family where matters can also get out of hand with tragic results. There is no substitute for intelligent administration. Cultural diversity in itself is not the cause of terror. Diversity has obvious political repercussions, but just as all politics do not end up in hostilities, cultural matters need not end up with Kalashnikovs. Terror, especially terror of the kind we have witnessed, is a profoundly political act with serious political implications and repercussions. It is intended to be so. It is said that war is an extension of diplomacy by other means. Similarly the use of terror is a kind of warfare by other means.

Robespierre in one of his speeches said that 'the main spring of popular government in time of revolution is both virtue and terror: virtue, without which terror is evil; terror, without which virtue is helpless. Terror is nothing but justice, prompt, severe and inflexible: it is therefore an emanation of virtue' (quoted by Elie Kedourie in *Nationalism in Asia and Africa* (London: Routledge, 1974), p.103).

Robespierre was formulating the use of terror by the state presumably for lofty ideals. All states claim the monopoly of force, and thereby the use of deadly weapons for their own purposes. We do not need to be reminded of Hiroshima and Nagasaki. When the state engages in terror to crush 'terrorists', as is often the case, then it is the very conception of justice which rises to the surface.

Terror in the hands of rebel groups is the problem in question. We may agree or disagree with the intentions of such groups. There is little doubt though that great states are formed, which began with the rebellion of small armed groups. The US is one example: Paul Revere and the actions of the rebellious group of people in Boston would have been regarded as terrorists in London. Israel came into being in 1948 after much illegal activity by underground armed forces both against the British administration in Palestine and against the UN. The Irgun and the Stern Gang, secretly supported from abroad, finally forced the British to give up the Mandate in Palestine through terrorist activity. Once Israel was recognized as a state, past members of these underground groups, Yitzak Shamir and Menahem Begin both became honoured prime ministers. So the nature of terrorist actions have to be examined in the context of the political circumstances that give rise to them. This does not mean that they can be excused. It only means that a political position must be formulated to deal with them. However much the Sinhalese may have referred to the Tamil Tigers as terrorists, a civil war of fifty years ensued which demanded a political solution.

The problem of terror before us is not cultural diversity. Terror arises out of political grievances. It is the sense of dishonour and injustice that drives people to undertake extreme actions as injured and victimized parties. After 9/11 there was much speculation whether the large Irish constituency in the US would regard the actions of the IRA in Northern Ireland as terrorism. The British had no doubts about it.

Cultural diversity is an essential ingredient of a modern, vibrant, creative society. It would be impossible to imagine Paris without a Picasso (Spaniard), Van Gogh (Dutch) or Nijinski and Nureyev (Russians). The vitality of the US is impossible to imagine without the contributions of the millions of gifted immigrants. Only in the last twenty years have the Indian immigrants put their mark on many American businesses – from the Patidar in hotels and motels, to the great entrepreneurs in information technology coming out of Indian technical colleges. We need hardly mention the immense contributions of Japanese, Chinese, Korean, Vietnamese and other Asians in the US. Terror is another matter altogether.

Terror and the clash of civilizations

Terror and cultural diversity is parallel to the problem of war and the 'clash of civilizations'. Here again, there is much loose talk these days about the great division between Islam and West. Bernard Lewis has written of the 'Revolt of Islam' (*New Yorker*, 19 November 2001). He had also written of the 'Roots of Islamic Rage' in which he predicted a coming clash of civilizations long before Samuel Huntington became the Cassandra of doom. 'When civilizations clash, there is one that prevails, and one that is shattered,' he wrote, and he added prophetically, 'the usual result of such an encounter is a cohabitation of the worst' (Bernard Lewis, *Middle East and the West* (Bloomington: Indiana University Press, 1964)). Edward Said and Roy Mottahedeh, to take two of the most prominent critics of Lewis and Huntington, have provided us with all the reasons why these thoughts are unfounded. Nonetheless, the suspicion persists that there must be some cultural incompatibility between Islam and the West which makes for a clash to seem inevitable. Osama bin Laden certainly was more in the 'Huntington' mode than Huntington himself. He would have wanted to play the role of the leader of a Universal Islam against the West.

Are we going to have a clash of civilizations á la Hollywood, as predicted by Osama bin Laden and Samuel Huntington? Is this going to be between Islam in general and the West, or only between Arabs and the Anglo-Americans? And who is going to lead it? Some lieutenant of Osama and his Wahhabi warriors? Saddam Hussein and his secular forces? Colonel Khaddafi supported by his oil fortunes paid for by Europe? Or perhaps will the forces of a militant Islam be led by President Khamenei of Iran? Even the mere mention of such names is likely to remind us of how preposterous these paranoid speculations turn out to be. There is now in the West a curious inchoate anxiety about a huge swath of mankind who, it is thought, is somehow out to destroy Western capitalist civilization. At least so writes, Paul Kennedy, the celebrated Yale historian in his review of the views of Bernard Lewis, in the *New York Times* Book Review of 27 January 2002:

> The unvarnished truth is that the tensions there are of a different order of magnitude . . . a vast, sprawling area, where a badly damaged though powerful and religiously driven order is locked in battle with global trends more penetrating and unsettling than could ever have been imagined . . . What Lewis is writing about . . . concerns one of the greatest cultural and political divides in modern history.

There has been nothing like this fear since the days of the Berlin or Cuban crisis and the Iron Curtain. We need to examine the basis for these exaggerated worries.

What is amazing is that this vague fear of terrorism is so much more acute in the US – with the most powerful military-industrial complex in the world – than in Europe, which, after all, is home to many millions of Muslims. Allow me to raise the question as to whether this is a matter of cultural difference or whether some of these Islamic countries have some good hard political reasons to detest the high-handed policies of the West.

Osama bin Laden in his 7 October videotape spoke of the 'more than eighty years' of 'humiliation and disgrace' suffered by Muslim peoples at the hands of Westerners. Many in the West wondered what he could have meant by that date, though in the Middle East his listeners could relate immediately to the cataclysmic events at the end of the First World War. In 1918, the last great Islamic state, the Ottoman Empire of 600 years, was defeated and its provinces divided up between fractious victorious powers who could hardly agree among themselves how to share the spoils. In 1924, the Turks, who had provided the military shield for the Islamic and Asian world, decided to cut their losses and go their own way. They abolished the ancient institution of the caliphate in 1924 which had provided a sense of unity to Islamic peoples. It has not been revived since.

These catastrophic events were followed by much further humiliation, especially for the Arab-speaking peoples. The Turks rejected their defeat. They fought back against the allies, won back their liberty, and reorganized themselves to form their secular republic. They have been cultivating their love affair with the West in NATO and in the Council of Europe ever since. The Arabs on the other hand were misled by their leaders, thoroughly double-crossed by the allies, led astray, broken up into various so-called 'protectorates' and finally totally dominated by Britain and France between the two world wars.

As if these colonial disasters were not enough of a punishment and a stern example to others in the British Empire, such as India, who might have entertained dangerous ideas of independence, Britain also decided to provide a 'homeland for Jews' in Palestine – an ancient land that was densely occupied by a rural population of mainly Arabic speakers. There were Jews among them, and Christians of various denominations. The majority, however, were Muslims.

Up to this point in the rich history of these lands no one in this vast region had been conscious of belonging to 'nations'. As far back as one could recall, all these peoples had been subjects of the sultan. It was the Ottoman sultan who had the duty to make sure that the subjects of his domain were contented and at peace with each other. And, indeed, a large degree of local autonomy and a general peace had reigned over these lands ever since the defeat of the Mamluk Turks of Egypt by the Ottoman Turks of the north in 1517. The peace had been punctuated, it is true, by local troubles from time to time, but these had been manageable. They had not led to large-scale national movements of any kind. The Middle East in this respect was unlike the troublesome Balkan lands in the nineteenth century where nationalist passions engendered by European ideological currents had been the order of the day.

With the defeat of the Ottomans, the British and the French proceeded with the effective policy of *divida et impera*. So, Iraq, Syria, Lebanon, Transjordan, Saudi Arabia and a multitude of small sheikdoms on the Persian-Arabian Gulf were created in the 1920s with entirely artificial borders which are still in dispute. The Kuwait affair in 1990 is part of this story. They were controlled by colonial officers through indirect rule. Egypt, occupied earlier, was constantly chafing against British rule, and there were many uprisings in Iraq, Syria, Palestine and elsewhere. Their troubles read like a depressing history of intrigue and deception between the colonial powers and the local populations.

Enter America. American anti-colonial influence, combined with the great oil discoveries in Saudi Arabia, eventually undermined British and French rule in the Middle East. The Suez War of 1956 was the last direct attempt by the old colonial powers to hold some military outposts in the region. Meanwhile, with the arrival of millions of Jews escaping from the racism and the unspeakable outrages of Europe, the Israel problem came to dominate Arab consciousness. The pitiful plight of the Palestinians, who had been chased out of their homes and villages with the creation of the State of Israel in 1948, could not be evaded. The continuing tragedy in Palestine began to haunt every Arab regime. It led to hopeless wars with Israel in which many thousands lost their lives.

Given all this sorry history, and the daily humiliation of Palestinians for the last fifty or more years, is it surprising

154

that some people have become desperate. Are American ambassadors not aware of the negative mood in Arab streets? How long is it going to be possible to control the ordinary people by rich and powerful elite groups? Franz Fanon wrote bitterly about the 'collaborating middle classes' in Africa in relation to white colonial rule. Similarly, the ordinary people in the Arab lands feel that their rulers have betrayed them.

Listen to the chief of intelligence in Saudi Arabia: the recent eloquent warnings of Prince Abdul Aziz, the director of the Saudi intelligence service, are quite telling. The *New York Times* (27 January 2002) reports that the prince indicated that, according to a Saudi intelligence survey, 'of educated Saudis between the ages of 25 and 41 . . . 95% of them supported Mr bin Laden's cause . . . even though they rejected the attacks in New York and Washington.' Arabs and many others in Iran, Pakistan and elsewhere are angry. 'All the governments, the people of the region believe that America is supporting Israel whether it is right or wrong, and now if something happens to Yasir Arafat, the feeling against American policy will be stronger.' He also had something quite pointed to say about American attitudes to the region. 'Some days you say you want to attack Iraq, some days Somalia, some days Lebanon, some days Syria,' he said. 'Who do you want to attack? All the Arab world? And you want us to support that? It's impossible. It's impossible.'

America had made this mistake before in Iran when it supported the Shah against the nationalist Mosaddeq. Eventually the Shah regime was destroyed by a popular revolution which took an Islamic form. Similarly, the popular feelings in Arab countries are also turning in the direction of Islam.

None of this has to do with the diversity of Islamic or Western civilization. It has everything to do with hard political facts on the ground in various parts of the world in which the US projects her power. The fight has nothing to do with Coca-Cola, but everything to do with the use of F-16s in Israel, and Apache helicopters in the Philippines. It is part of the concern, which is widely shared, with the use being made of the overwhelming military, economic and political instruments in order to control the fate of entire nations. The temptation is towards a new *imperium*. We are now facing great dangers in the creation of a more equitable and peaceful world. We will need much greater international cooperation and much more effective international institutions. There is no question that better and more statesmanlike policies – not simple-minded slogans – are needed to solve the urgent problems that confront us.

Lévi-Strauss warned us fifty years ago with some memorable lines on this subject of diversity:

> The necessity of preserving the diversity of cultures in a world which is threatened by monotony and uniformity has surely not remained unnoticed by international institutions ... We must listen to wheat growing, encourage secret potentialities, awaken all the vocations to live together that history holds in reserve ... Tolerance is not a contemplative position, dispensing indulgence to what was and to what is. It is a dynamic attitude, consisting in the foresight, the understanding and promotion of what wants to be. The diversity of human cultures is behind us, around us and ahead of us. The only demand that we may make upon it (creating for each individual corresponding duties) is that it realize itself in forms such that each is a contribution to the greater generosity of the others. (in 'Race and History', *Structural Anthropology*, Volume 2, 1958).

Cambridge, 23 February 2002

Glossary

Abū Rayhān al-Bīrūnī (973–1048), Persian scientist and historian; author of books on ethnology, geography and historical science of Central Asia and India.

Académie Française, or the French Academy, the oldest academy of the Institut de France; founded for the purpose of editing the French dictionary and formalizing French grammar.

Ahimsa, a Sanskrit term meaning non-violence; an important tenet common to Buddhism, Jainism and Hinduism that teaches not to kill or injure living beings.

Alexander the Great (356–323 BCE), king of Macedon; conquered Syria, Egypt and Persia; created the Hellenistic cultural foundation.

Altaic languages, a language family distributed widely in Southern Siberia, Mongolia, Central Asia, north-eastern China, etc.; some linguists include Korean and Japanese.

Ankara University, founded by Mustafa Kemal Atatürk, the first president of the Republic of Turkey; one of the most prestigious universities in Turkey, with fifteen faculties, seven graduate schools and twenty-five research centres.

King Ashoka (304 BCE–232 BCE), the third incumbent of the Mauryan throne; ruled India and promoted Buddhism; led the Council of Pātaliputra in 250 BCE.

Atatürk, Mustafa Kemal (1881–1938), revived his country when the Ottoman Empire collapsed after the First World War; founded the Republic of Turkey; called 'Father of Turks'.

Aya Sophya Museum (Hagia Sophia [holy wisdom]), constructed in the fourth century as a church and reconstructed in the sixth century; became a mosque after the Byzantine Empire's fall; now a museum famous for its massive dome.

Bhakti, a word of Sanskrit origin meaning devotion; within Hinduism the word is used exclusively to indicate devotion to a particular deity or form of God.

King Bhumibol Adulyadej (b.1927), the current king of Thailand; reigned since coronation in 1946 at the age of eighteen; immensely popular and respected in Thailand.

Boston Research Center for the 21st Century, founded in 1993; works to build cultures of peace through dialogue and educational programmes, including public forums and scholarly seminars.

Buddagaya, the place in north-east India where Shakyamuni attained enlightenment.

Buddha, refers to one who has become awakened to the ultimate truth of all phenomena in Buddhism and at first was applied exclusively to Shakyamuni, the founder of Buddhism.

Caucasia, a region in Eurasia between the Great Caucasus mountain range and the Lesser Caucasus Mountains; bordered on the west by the Black Sea and on the east by the Caspian Sea.

Chang-an or the Great Teacher Chang-an (561–632), born in China; became a disciple of Tiantai; recorded Tiantai's three major works: *The Words and Phrases of the Lotus Sutra*, *The Profound Meaning of the Lotus Sutra* and *Great Concentration and Insight*.

Chowdhury, Anwarul K. (b.1943), under-secretary-general of the United Nations (2002–7); served as president of the Security Council, president of the United Nations Children's Fund (UNICEF) executive board and vice-president of the Economic and Social Council of the UN in 1997 and 1998.

Comte, Auguste (1798–1857), French thinker; known as the father of sociology; author of *Cours de Philosophie Positive.*

Cyrillic alphabet, used in Slavic languages such as Russian, Bulgarian, Macedonian, Serbian and other languages of the former Soviet Union.

Demirel, Süleyman (b.1924), Turkish politician; the ninth president of the Republic of Turkey (1993–2000).

Dome of the Rock, the oldest Muslim building in Jerusalem, which encloses a huge rock located at its centre, from which, according to tradition, the Prophet Muhammad ascended to heaven.

Dumas, Alexandre (1802–70), French writer and playwright; most popular in nineteenth-century France; author of *The Count of Monte Cristo* and *The Three Musketeers*.

Durkheim, Émile (1858–1917), a French sociologist and an educator; formed the Durkheimian School; author of *The Division of Labour in Society* and *Elementary Forms of the Religious Life*.

Eisenhower, Dwight David (1890–1969), American soldier and politician; Supreme Commander of the Allied forces in Europe during the Second World War; thirty-fourth president of the United States (1953–61).

Emre, Yunus (c.1238–c.1321), Turkish poet who created homely poems on the theme of Turkish people's life; said to have been influenced by Islamic mysticism.

Enkhbayar, Nambaryn (b.1958), Mongolian politician; prime minister of Mongolia (2000–4); current president of Mongolia.

European Academy of Sciences and Arts, founded in 1990 by Dr Felix Unger and other scientists; with a membership of approximately 1,300 scientists and artists in Europe.

European Court of Human Rights, instituted as a permanent court in November 1998 to protect the Convention for the Protection of Human Rights and Fundamental Freedoms that entered into force in 1953.

February 26 Incident, the coup d'état in Tokyo on 26 February 1936; attempted by young army officers; suppressed on 29 February.

Gandhi, Mohandas Karamchand, 'Mahatma Gandhi' (1869–1948), leader of the Indian nationalist movement against British rule; esteemed for his doctrine of non-violent protest; Mahatma is a designation meaning 'Great Soul'.

Gökalp, Ziya (1876–1924), leading thinker and Turkish nationalist.

Gopi, a word originally meaning 'cow-herd girl' in Sanskrit.

Gorbachev, Mikhail (b.1931), the former general secretary of the Soviet Communist Party and the last president of the Soviet

Union; awarded the Nobel Peace Prize (1990) for his diplomacy leading to the end of the Cold War.

Hagia Irene Museum (temple to peace), the oldest church in Istanbul; constructed in the era of the Eastern Roman Empire (395–1453); located between the Aya Sophya Museum and the Topkapi Palace.

El Hassan bin Talal, Prince of Jordan (b.1947), the former president of the Club of Rome and the supreme adviser to the European Academy of Sciences and Arts; specializes in the fields of peace, human rights and education.

Hikmet, Nazim (1902–63), Turkish poet and pacifist, arrested and imprisoned for a total of seventeen years; created poems, novels, essays and plays in prison.

Ibn Rushd (1126–98), Arab Aristotelian scholar and Islamic philosopher whose name was Latinized as 'Averroes'.

Ibn Sina (980–1037), Arab Aristotelian scholar and Islamic philosopher whose name was Latinized as 'Avicenna'.

Institute of Oriental Philosophy, established in 1962; directs research in the history, literature and concepts of Buddhism and other religions; hosts a series of symposia and public lectures.

International Criminal Court, established in 2002 as a permanent tribunal to prosecute individuals for genocide, crimes against humanity, war crimes and the crime of aggression; located in The Hague, Netherlands.

Issues of global concern; the common concerns of human beings; issues that are related to food, energy, environment, poverty, human rights and nuclear weaponry.

Kemal, Namik (1840–88), poet and intellectual leader at the end of the Ottoman Empire.

Kemal, Yaşar (b.1922), an exponent of modern Turkish writers; author of *Memed, My Hawk*.

Kokin Wakashū (Collected Japanese Poems from Ancient and Modern Times), the first collection of Japanese poetry, compiled at the emperor's request.

Krieger, David (b.1942), president of the Nuclear Age Peace Foundation; declared conscientious objection to conscription; co-author with Daisaku Ikeda of *Choose Hope: Your Role in Waging Peace in the Nuclear Age*.

Krishna, a deity worshipped across many traditions of Hinduism.

Lévi-Strauss, Claude (b.1908), French anthropologist; developed structuralism to explain the structure of human culture.

Lewis, Bernard (b.1916), English historian and an honorary professor of Princeton University; author of *What Went Wrong?: Western Impact and Middle Eastern Response* and *The Crisis of Islam: Holy War and Unholy Terror*.

Lu Xun (1881–1936), Chinese writer; author of *A Madman's Diary* and *The True Story of Ah Q*.

Magna Carta, 1215 charter granting civil and political liberties to the people of England; influenced the development of many constitutional documents.

Makiguchi, Tsunesaburo (1871–1944), educator, founder-president of Soka Gakkai and author of *Education for Creative Living* and *A Geography of Human Life*.

Man'yōshū (Collection of Ten Thousand Leaves), the oldest existing collection of approximately 4,500 Japanese poems created by people of various ranks including the emperor, aristocrats and soldiers in Japan from the end of the seventh century to the eighth century.

Mao Zedong (1893–1976), a Chinese military and political leader who led the Communist Party of China (CPC); became the leader of the People's Republic of China (PRC) from its establishment in 1949 until his death; the Cultural Revolution was one of his social-political programmes.

Maududi, Sayyid Abul A'la (1903–79), born in colonial India; Pakistani journalist, theologist and political philosopher; founder and president of the Jamaat-e-Islami Islamic political party (established in 1941).

McCarthyism (also called the 'Red Scare'), a term describing the intense anti-communist suspicion in the United States in a period that lasted roughly from the late 1940s to the late 1950s; originally coined to criticize the actions of US Senator Joseph McCarthy.

Military-industrial complex, combination of the United States' armed forces, arms industry and associated political and commercial interests.

Mongol invasions of Japan, two major military operations undertaken by Kublai Khan of the Mongol Empire to invade the Japanese islands in 1274 and 1281.

Mōri Motonari (1497–1571), a general in the Warring State period of Japanese history; active in the Chugoku District, the south-western part of Japan.

Nanda, Ved Prakash (b.1934), Indian legal scholar and president of the World Association of Law Professors; also vice provost for the School of Law, University of Denver; co-author with Daisaku Ikeda of *The Spirit of India – Buddhism and Hinduism: A Dialogue*.

Nichiren (1222–82), Japanese Buddhist prophet; founder of Nichiren Buddhism, which reveres the teachings of the Lotus Sutra.

Ortega y Gasset, José (1883–1955), Spanish philosopher who greatly influenced Spain's twentieth-century cultural and literary renaissance.

Özal, Turgut (1927–93), Turkish politician; the eighth president of the Republic of Turkey (1989–93).

Pamuk, Orhan (b.1952), awarded the Nobel Prize in Literature in 2006 for his memoir *Istanbul*; author of *The Silent House*, *The Black Book* and other novels.

Pascal, Blaise (1623–62), French scientist and philosopher; formulator of Pascal's theorem; author of *Pensées*.

Pauling, Linus (1901–94), noted for his studies on molecular structure and chemical bonding; an early advocate of the health benefits of large doses of vitamin C; awarded the Nobel Prize for Chemistry (1954) and the Nobel Peace Prize (1962) for his efforts on behalf of nuclear weapons control; co-author with Daisaku Ikeda of *A Lifelong Quest for Peace*.

Pugwash Conferences on Science and World Affairs; international organization of scholars and public figures founded in 1957 by Joseph Rotblat and Bertrand Russell in Pugwash, Canada, to reduce the danger of armed conflict and to seek solutions to global security; Pugwash Conferences and Rotblat jointly won Nobel Peace Prize in 1995 for their efforts towards nuclear disarmament.

Rotblat, Joseph (1908–2005), one of the scientists recruited to the Manhattan Project; turned his back on the project and became a campaigner for the abolition of nuclear weapons; co-founder of the Pugwash Conferences on Science and World

Affairs; awarded the Nobel Peace Prize (1995), co-author with Daisaku Ikeda of *A Quest for Global Peace*.

Rousseau, Jean-Jacques (1712–78), French philosopher; his political ideas influenced the French Revolution; author of *Du Contrat Social, Principes du Droit Politique* and *Émile*.

Rumi, Jalal al-Din (1207–73), Persian poet and Sufi philosopher; his work *Masnavi* is counted as one of the masterpieces of Sufi literature.

Said, Edward (1935–2003), Palestinian writer; author of *Orientalism* and *Culture and Imperialism*.

San Francisco Peace Conference, held 4–8 September 1951 in San Francisco, California; officially called Treaty of Peace with Japan; signed by forty-nine nations on 8 September.

Shi'ite, also Shī'a (Arabic, 'party'), Muslims who believe that Alī was the legitimate successor to Muhammad; Shī'a communities form the majority in Iran and parts of Iraq.

Soka Gakkai, Buddhist organization founded in Japan in 1930 and formally inaugurated in 1937; the society follows the teachings of Nichiren, based on the Lotus Sutra's philosophy of compassion.

Soka Gakkai International, Buddhist association with more than 12 million members in 192 countries and territories worldwide; the promotion of peace, culture and education is central to Soka Gakkai International's activities.

Spengler, Oswald (1880–1936), German philosopher and writer; predicted the eclipse of Western civilization in *Der Utergang des Abendlandes* (The Decline of the West).

Sufis, Muslims who seek close, direct and personal experience of God; their practice is described as Islamic mysticism.

Suleiman I (1494–1566), the tenth sultan of the Ottoman Empire; ruled the empire from 1520 to 1566 and made it most prosperous; reconstructed its legal system.

Suleiman's Mosque, a grand mosque in Istanbul that was built by the order of the Suleiman I of the Ottoman Empire.

Sultan, the title used by the rulers of the Muslim dynasty after the eleventh century.

Tagore, Rabindranath (1861–1941), Bengali poet, writer, composer and painter; author of *Gitanjali*; awarded the Nobel Prize for Literature in 1913.

Tehranian, Majid (b.1937), former professor of international communications at the University of Hawaii and director of the Toda Institute for Global Peace and Policy Research (1996–2008); co-author with Daisaku Ikeda of *Global Civilization, A Buddhist–Islamic Dialogue*.

Theravada, an early school of Buddhism; the form of Buddhism prevalent in Sri Lanka and South-East Asia.

Toda, Josei (1900–58), Japanese educator, philosopher and the second president of Soka Gakkai; a direct disciple of the founding president, Tsunesaburo Makiguchi, and mentor of the third president, Daisaku Ikeda.

Toda Institute for Global Peace and Policy Research, founded in 1996; offices in Tokyo and Honolulu; sponsors research programmes on global peace and human security policy issues.

Topkapi Palace, the official residence of the Ottoman sultans in Istanbul from 1465 to 1853; made up of many small buildings and gardens.

Toynbee, Arnold J. (1889–1975), English historian best known for his twelve-volume *A Study of History*; co-author with Daisaku Ikeda of *Choose Life: A Dialogue*.

Treaty against Nuclear Terrorism, an international treaty to fight nuclear terrorism perpetrated through possession of atomic devices or radioactive materials; approved by the UN General Assembly in April 2005.

Treaty of Sèvres, peace treaty concluded at Sèvres, France, in 1920 between the Allied Powers and the Ottoman Empire; solidified the partitioning of the Ottoman Empire.

Treaty of Versailles, peace treaty concluded at Château de Versailles in 1919 between the Allied and Associated Powers and Germany to end the First World War.

Tughril Beg (c.993–1063), founder of the Turkish Seljuk sultanate; attempted to unite the Islamic world in Eurasia.

Tulip Age, period when tulips were the craze in upper-class society during the prosperous reign of Ahmed III of the Ottoman Empire (1703–30); popular complaints and rebellions resulted in the decline of the age.

Turkish Seljuk Empire, established by Tughril Beg who was a descendant of Seljuk and leader of Turkish mercenaries in the eastern part of Iran in mid-eleventh century; Persianized in cultures and language; the Seljuk dynasty reigned until 1308.

United Nations Peace-Building Commission, a 'UN reform' established in December 2005 by the United Nations General Assembly and the Security Council.

United Nations Human Rights Council, an international body established in March 2006 within the United Nations System; addresses human rights violations.

Wahid, Abdurrahman (b.1940), born in Java, Indonesia; served as the chairman of Nahdlatul Ulama (independent Islamic organization); the fourth president of Indonesia (1999–2001).

Wickramasinghe, Chandra (b.1939), Sri Lankan astronomer; professor of applied mathematics and astronomy at the University of Wales, Cardiff; co-author with Daisaku Ikeda of *Space and Eternal Life*.

Zhou Enlai (1898–1976), a prominent Communist Party of China leader; premier of the People's Republic of China from 1949 until his death in January 1976; as a student at Nankai University, he took part in the revolutionary May Fourth Movement.

Ziya Pasha (1825–80), man of letters and politician at the end of the Ottoman Empire; contributed to innovation in the Turkish language and literature.

Zweig, Stefan (1881–1942), Austrian novelist; exiled to Brazil to escape from persecution by Nazi Germany; author of *Joseph Fouché* and *Marie Antoinette*.

Notes

Chapter 1

1 Yunus Emre, trans. Sühasaiz, *The City of the Heart: Yunus Emre's Verses of Wisdom and Love* (Rockport: Element Books, 1992), p.59.
2 Arnold J. Toynbee, *Acquaintances* (Oxford: Oxford University Press, 1967), p.248.
3 Ibid., p.241.
4 *The Writings of Nichiren Daishonin* (Tokyo: Soka Gakkai, 1999), p.141.

Chapter 2

1 *The Writings of Nichiren Daishonin* (Tokyo: Soka Gakkai, 1999), p.955.
2 Ibid., p.497.
3 Ibid., p.16.

Chapter 3

1 Arnold J. Toynbee, *The World and the West* (London: London University Press, 1953), p.28.
2 H.C. Armstrong, *Grey Wolf* (London: Arthur Barker Ltd, 1938), p.285.

Chapter 4

1 *The Collected Works of Mahatma Gandhi*, (Delhi: Publications Division, Ministry of Information and Broadcasting, Government of India, September 1927–January 1928), p.250.
2 Claude Lévi-Strauss, *Race et Histoire*, (Paris: Unesco, 1952), published in a report devoted to the battle against racism.

Chapter 6

1 *The Record of the Orally Transmitted Teachings* (Tokyo: Soka Gakkai, 2004), p.146.
2 Ibid., p.11.

Chapter 7

1 Bernard Lewis, *The Jews of Islam* (Princeton, NJ: Princeton University Press, 1984), pp.135–6.
2 *The Record of the Orally Transmitted Teachings* (Tokyo: Soka Gakkai, 2004), p.165.
3 Linus Pauling and Daisaku Ikeda, *A Lifelong Quest for Peace* (Boston: Jones and Bartlett Publishers, Inc., 1992), pp.94–5.

Chapter 10

1 Arnold J. Toynbee and Daisaku Ikeda, *Choose Life* (Oxford: Oxford University Press, 1989), p.90.

Appendix 1

1 Talat Sait Halam, *The Humanist Poetry of Yunus Emre* (Istanbul: Istanbul Matbaasi, 1972), p.78.
2 Arnold J. Toynbee, *The World and the West* (London: Oxford University Press, 1953), p.28.
3 Ibid., p.29.
4 Daisaku Ikeda, *Songs from My Heart: The People*, trans. Burton Watson (New York and Tokyo: John Weatherhill Inc., 1978), pp.75–6.

5   David Hotham, *The Turks* (London: John Murray Ltd, 1972), p.24.
6   Simone Weil, *The Need for Roots* (London: Ark Paperbacks, 1987), p.105.
7   Yunus Emre, trans. Sühasaiz, *The City of the Heart: Yunus Emre's Verses of Wisdom and Love* (Rockport: Element Books, 1992), p.59.

Index

Abdul Aziz, Prince 155
Abū Rayhān al-Birūnī 51, 157
Académie Française 157
Afghanistan 82, 149
ageing 80–1, 86
ahimsa 97, 157
al-Qaeda 142, 149
Alexander the Great 4, 157
alms 93
Altaic languages 5, 157
Anguttara-nikāya 81
Ankara 41
Ankara University 1, 131, 157
anthropology *see* cultural
    anthropology
Armenian genocide 125–6
Ashoka, Mauryan King of India 17,
    18, 158
Atatürk, Mustafa Kemal
  character and values 133–4,
    137–8
  on importance of people 135
  influence on Japan 28
  influences 138
  on international humanism 44,
    45–6
  on leadership 42
  modern reputation 41–2
  monuments to 14
  overview 158
  reforms 33–42, 43, 133–9

Atatürk Mausoleum 41
Averroes (Ibn Rushd) 51, 68, 161
Avicenna (Ibn Sina) 51, 161

Baghdad 147, 148
Balkans 69, 115, 143, 154
Bangkok 3
Barth, Fredrik 80
bathing 24
Begin, Menahem 150
bhakti 95, 158
Bhumibol Adulyadej, King of
    Thailand 3, 158
bin Laden, Osama 149, 152, 155
The Black Tulip (Dumas) 8
Boston Research Center for the 21st
    Century xi, 45, 114, 158
Britain
  2005 bombings 102
  and Islamic world 41, 63, 67
  and Middle East 153, 154
  Yalman's experience of 74
Buddagaya 158
Buddha 16, 113, 114, 158
Buddhism
  and compassion 95
  current rise 65
  and death 86
  humanism of 81–2, 87–8, 113
  and importance of actions 114,
    127

Mahayana 86, 87
as peace promoter 15–18
prayers 15
and reciprocal respect 96
respect for life 97
on self and others 77
in Sri Lanka 75–6
Theravada 75–6, 166
and understanding other cultures
53

Calais 145–6
Caucasia 158
Chang-an 159
children: games 24
China 35, 109–10, 168
Chowdhury, Anwarul K. 99, 159
Christianity
dangers of evangelizing tradition
17–18
fundamentalism 91
Jesus' love of the world 95
persecution of Jews 89–90
CIA 67
civilization: and progress 137
civilizations see cultures and
civilizations
coffee 4, 22
colonialism, Western 27–8, 52–3,
55, 67, 153–6
commerce: negotiating prices
12–13
Comte, Auguste 36, 159
Constantinople see Istanbul
consumerism 86
Cordoba 68
cosmology see mythology
Crusades 115
cultural anthropology
definition x, 50–1
and empathy 44
and globalization 54–5
good fieldwork practice 79–80
history of 51–3
and overcoming prejudice 55–9,
61–2, 73–4
see also Lévi-Strauss, Claude
cultural diversity

Istanbul ix, 2–4, 24, 74, 89, 90, 120
need for intercultural dialogue
61–72, 100–1
need for interfaith dialogue 78,
80, 85–6, 114, 116, 128
need for respect for 44
obsession with difference 87
peaceful management 69, 89–90,
146–9, 150–1, 153–4
and terrorism 141–55
see also stereotyping
cultures and civilizations
promoting peace through mutual
comprehension 61–72
rise and decline 62–5
stereotypical views 63–4, 68, 70,
142
West's sense of superiority 52,
55–9
Cyrillic alphabet 40, 159

death 81–2, 86–7
Demirel, Süleyman 26–7, 159
Diderot, Denis 51
differences see cultural diversity
Dome of the Rock 114, 159
Dostoyevsky, Fyodor 52
Dumas, Alexandre 8, 159
Durkheim, Émile 113, 159

earthquakes 22, 142
Edirne letter 89–90
education 38–40, 119–26, 136–7
Egypt 154
Eisenhower, Dwight D. 122, 160
El Hassan bin Talal, Prince of
Jordan 85, 94, 161
Elizabeth I, Queen of England 24
empathy: developing 80–2
Emre, Yunus 1, 9, 132, 139, 160
Enkhbayar, Nambaryn 20, 160
equality: and Islam 93–4
Ertugrul Firkateyni (ship) 21
European Academy of Sciences and
Arts 160, 161
European Court of Human Rights
106, 160
European Union 33, 90

family life 104
Fanon, Franz 155
festivals 13
Finley, Moses 143
First World War 43, 125–6, 153
flags 4
flowers 7–8
France 63, 67, 145–6, 154
French Enlightenment 51
French Revolution 138, 149–50
funerals 13–14

games 24
Gandhi, Mohandas K. ('Mahatma')
    31, 52, 83, 92, 160
Germany 42–3, 142
globalization 54–5, 65–6, 70, 128
Goethe, Johann Wolfgang von 52
Gogol, Nikolai 52
Gökalp, Ziya 36, 160
Gopis 95, 160
Gorbachev, Mikhail S. 125, 160–1
gravestones 14

Hajj 15
Hashimoto, Kingoro 28
Hegel, Georg Wilhelm Friedrich 52
Herodotus 51
Hikmet, Nazim 9, 161
Hinduism 65, 75, 95
Hiroshima 9
history: importance of studying
    125–6
Hitler, Adolf 42, 43, 134
Holocaust 115
human rights 106–7
humanism
    definition 85
    universal 44–6
Huntington, Samuel P. 66, 68,
    151–2

Ibn Batuta 149
Ibn Khurradadhbeh 148
Ibn Rushd see Averroes
Ibn Sina see Avicenna
ICC see International Criminal
    Court

ICSAIT see International
    Convention for the Suppression
    of Acts of International
    Terrorism
Ikeda, Daisaku
    in Iran 28
    speeches by x, 2, 131–9
    visit to Yalman's home x, 2
illness 81–2
imperialism see colonialism
India 41, 120, 144–5, 146, 151
individualism 104
İnönü İsmet 135
Institute of Oriental Philosophy
    114, 161
International Convention for
    the Suppression of Acts
    of International Terrorism
    (ICSAIT) 105
International Criminal Court (ICC)
    105, 161
IRA 150
Iran
    Ikeda's experience 28
    and intercultural dialogue 101
    Islamic government 37–8
    Islamic revolution (1979) 155
    and Soviet Union 40
    and the West 41
Iran–Iraq War 21–2
Iraq
    Baghdad in first millennium 147,
        148
    Sunni–Shi'a conflict 115
    Western aggression 41
    Western creation of artificial state
        154
    Western occupation 55, 82
Islam
    Atatürk's reputation among
        Muslims 41–2
    attitude to monasticism and
        priestly orders 81
    cultural influence 92
    current rise 64–5
    and divine love 95–6
    festivals and celebrations 13

fundamentalist 63
funerals 13–14
knowledge of in Japan 6, 91–2
Koran 10, 114
Muslims in former Yugoslavia
    143–4
Muslims in India 145
and other religions 69, 89–90, 114
Ottoman Empire's role 148,
    153–4
overview of beliefs 92–4
prayers and religious rituals
    14–15
relationship between secular and
    religious power 37–8
respect for human life 97–8
and science 94
sense of one Muslim nation
    147–9
Shi'ites 115, 165
Sufis 15, 95–6, 165
Sunnis 115
things could teach the West and
    vice versa 71
trade and travel among Muslim
    countries 147–9
treatment of women 10–12
and Turkish politics 42
West's relationship with 41, 62–3,
    66–9, 82–3, 91, 101, 151–5
world population xi, 92
Israel
    creation of 150, 153
    Palestine conflict 92, 102, 154
    US support for 155
Istanbul
    Aya Sophya Museum 3–4, 158
    Bosporus bridges xii
    cultural diversity ix, 2–4, 24, 74,
        89, 90, 120
    Hagia Irene Museum 4, 161
    Suleiman's Mosque 3, 166
    Topkapi Palace 4, 161, 167

Japan
    bathing customs 24
    character traits 27, 48, 132
    children's games 24

dance 49–50
education 30, 122
favourite flowers 7–8
February 26 Incident (1936) 28,
    160
festivals 13
flag 4
and globalization 65
gravestones 14
historical relations with Turkey
    19–22
and humane support activities 31
influence 120–1
internationalism 32
Japanese language 23–4
knowledge of Islam 6, 91–2
leadership 31–2
literature 9, 161, 162
Meiji Restoration 36
militarism 127
modernization 29
Mongol invasions 19–20, 163
music and singers 48–50
Osaka 12
preservation of traditional culture
    30
price negotiation 12
proverbs 25
relations with China 109–10
resistance of Western imperialism
    28
similarities between Japanese and
    Turkish 5–6, 23–4, 131–2
Tokyo 3
Tokyo earthquake 142
treatment of women 11, 38
Jerusalem 114, 159
Jesus Christ 95
Jews 68–9, 89, 115, 148, 153, 154

Kemal, Mustafa see Atatürk,
    Mustafa Kemal
Kemal, Namik 36, 161
Kemal, Yaşar 9, 162
Kennedy, Paul 152
Khomeini, Ayatollah Ruhollah 37
Khurelbaatar, Sodovjamtsyn 102–3
Kitab al-Hind 51

Kokin Wakashū 9, 162
Koran 10, 114
Krieger, David 99, 162
Krishna 95, 162
Kurds 125–6
Kuwait 154

languages and scripts 5, 22–4,
    39–40, 157, 159
leaders and leadership 25, 31–2, 42
Lebanon 154
Lévi-Strauss, Claude
    on empathy 80
    on history as mythology 126
    on humanism 111, 113
    and the Japanese 30
    on mythology 56–9, 111
    overview 162
    on primitivism 55–9, 76
    on tolerance x, 44, 156
Lewis, Bernard
    core ideas 62–3, 151
    influence 62
    on Jews in Ottoman Empire
        89–90
    Kennedy on views 152
    overview 162
    on trade in Muslim world 147,
        148
Libya 41
literature 8–10
loyalty 27
Lu Xun 34, 162

Magna Carta 162
Mahavagga 81
Makiguchi, Tsunesaburo
    and education 39
    on humanitarian competition 31,
        94
    importance and contemporaries
        34
    imprisonment and death 123
    on judging without
        understanding 6, 77
    on nationalism 103
    overview 162
Manço, Barış 47–8

Mansur, Abbasid caliph 147
Man'yōshū 9, 162
Mao Zedong 93, 163
Marmara Project xii
Maududi, Sayyid Abul A'la 93, 163
Maybury-Lewis, David 58
McCarthyism 142–3, 163
Middle East 92, 102, 153–5
    see also Palestine
Mikasa, Prince 29
Min-On Concert Association 5–6,
    47, 49
minorities: persecution of 82
modernization 29
Mongols 19–20, 163
monuments and memorials 14
Mōri Motonari 5, 163
Mottahedeh, Roy 151
Muhammad, Prophet 114, 159
music and singers 47–50
Mussolini, Benito 42, 134
mythology 56–9, 111–12

Nanda, Ved 99, 163
nationalism 102–3, 115
Netherlands 8
Nichiren 15, 20, 77, 127, 164
nightingales 7–8
9/11 82–3, 101, 141–2
Noda, Masaaki 79
Nogi, General Maresuke 30
nuclear weapons 97, 100, 105, 167

oil 41, 154
Orientalism (Said) 52–3, 63
Ortega y Gasset, José 117, 164
Osaka 12
Ottoman Empire
    and coherence of Islamic lands
        148, 153–4
    end of 35–6, 152–3
    political and religious authority
        37
    religious toleration 69, 89–90
    Tulip Age 8, 167
Ottoman Union 36
Out of Place (Said) 69–70
Özal, Turgut 21–2, 33, 164

Pajic (Balkan professor) 143
Pakistan 82–3
Palestine 69–70, 92, 102, 153, 154
Pamuk, Orhan 9, 164
Paris 151
Pascal, Blaise 50, 164
Pauling, Linda 88
Pauling, Linus 88, 97, 164
Pauling, Peter 88
Picasso, Pablo 34
Pickens, Laurence 49
poetry 9
popular culture 98
poverty 81–2
prayers 14–15
prices: negotiating 12–13
primitivism: Lévi-Strauss' dismissal
    of 55–9, 76
progress 104–5
proverbs 25–6
Pugwash Conferences on Science
    and World Affairs 100, 164
Pushkin, Alexander 52

racism 90–1
Railway Bosporus Tube Passage xii
Ramadan 15
reason: and Islam 94
religion
    and conflict 92, 103–4, 112–13,
        115–16
    divine love 95
    and education 123, 126
    ethical aspect 112
    and fanaticism 127–8
    in former Yugoslavia 115
    and humanism 85
    identity aspect 112–13, 115–16
    and modern loneliness 104
    need for interfaith dialogue 78,
        80, 85–6, 114, 116, 128
    need for the religious to mix with
        ordinary people 81
    role and value 77, 80, 88, 103–4,
        111–14, 116, 127
    in Sri Lanka 78
    toleration in Ottoman Empire 69,
        89–90

Turkey 13–15, 16, 37–8
    see also Buddhism; Christianity;
        Hinduism; Islam
responsiveness 26–7
Revere, Paul 150
Robespierre, Maximilien de 149–50
roses 7–8
Rotblat, Joseph 100, 164
Rousseau, Jean-Jacques 44, 51, 80,
    103, 116, 165
Rumi, Jalal al-Din 6, 9, 49, 50, 96,
    165
Russell, Bertrand 164
Russo-Japanese War (1904–5) 30

Said, Edward W. 52–3, 63, 69–70,
    151, 165
San Francisco Peace Conference
    (1951) 75, 165
Saudi Arabia 14, 154, 155
scapegoating 68, 142
science 94
scripts see languages and scripts
Second World War 125
Seljuks 5, 167
Seneca 68
Serin, Dr Necdet 132
Sèvres, Treaty of (1920) 43, 167
shakuhachi 49–50
Shakyamuni 75, 81, 87, 158
Shamir, Yitzak 150
Shi'ites 115, 165
Siddhartha, Prince 82, 86
singers see music and singers
Society for Value-Creating
    Education 39
Soka Gakkai and International
    and earthquake relief 22
    and education 38–9, 123, 124
    inspirations 123
    and interfaith dialogue 114
    internationalism 32
    members' way of life 126–7
    overview 165
    and parochial religious authority
        81
    Pauling exhibition 88
    and peace 15–18

and the UN 106, 132
women's role 38
worldwide presence 16
Soka University 109, 110, 121
Soka University of America (SUA)
    19, 121
Soviet Union 40
Spain: historical religious toleration
    68
Spengler, Oswald 62, 137, 165
Sri Lanka 74–8, 120, 144, 150
Srimala Sutra 77
Stalin, Joseph 42, 134
stereotyping: dangers of 63–4, 68,
    70, 142
SUA *see* Soka University of America
Suez War (1956) 154
Sufis 15, 95–6, 166
Suleiman I, Ottoman sultan 16
sultans 166
Sunnis 115
Syria 154

Tagore, Rabindranath 123–4, 166
Tehranian, Majid
    on alms 93
    background 28
    on ignorance of Islamic culture
        67, 91
    and Ikeda 28, 85
    and intercultural dialogue 100–1
    overview 166
terrorism
    causes 141–55
    and cultural diversity 141–55
    9/11 82–3, 101, 141–2
    post 9/11 102
    rejection of 67, 82
    and state formation 150
    state use of terror 149–50
    UN measures 105, 167
Thailand 3, 27–8
Thucydides 51
Tiantai 159
Toda, Josei
    on coups d'état 28
    and dialogue xii
    and education 39

imprisonment 123
on leaders 26
on nuclear weapons 97
overview 166
on solving humanity's problems
    70
Toda Institute for Global Peace and
    Policy Research xi, 45, 99–101,
    114, 166
Tōgō, Marshal Heihachirō 30
Tokyo 3, 142
Tolstoy, Leo 52
Toynbee, Arnold J.
    on civilizations 62
    on death 86
    on education 122
    on human history 129
    and Ikeda 26
    importance and contemporaries
        34
    on modern challenges 65
    overview 167
    and Turkey 6, 34–5, 133–4, 135
trade: among Muslim countries
    147–8
Transjordan 154
Treaty against Nuclear Terrorism
    105, 167
Tughril Beg 5, 167
La Tulipe Noire (Dumas) 8
tulips 8, 167
Turkey
    Ankara 41
    Ankara University 1, 157
    Atatürk's reforms 33–42, 43,
        133–9
    bathing customs 24
    character traits 26–7, 48, 132
    children's games 24
    dance 49–50
    earthquakes 22
    education 38–9, 136–7
    and EU membership 33
    European massacres in 6
    favourite flowers 7–8
    festivals 13
    and First World War 43, 125–6

flag 4
food 4
formation of republic 35–6, 153
funerals and gravestones 13–14
historical relations with Japan
    19–22
impressions of Japanese 29
Islamists in politics 42
legal system 106
literature 8–10
modern philosophy 133–9
modernization 29–30, 33–42
music and singers 47–50
prayers and religious rituals
    14–15
price negotiation 12
proverbs 25–6
religion 13–15, 16, 37–8
resistance of Western imperialism
    28
script change 39–40
similarities between Turkish and
    Japanese 5–6, 23–4, 131–2
treatment of women 10–12, 34, 38
Turkish language 23–4, 39–40
see also Istanbul

United Nations (UN)
    Alliance of Civilizations initiative
        71–2
    Human Rights Council 106, 168
    importance 83, 132
    and peace 105–7, 132
    Peace-Building Commission 105,
        106, 167
    reforming 100
    World Programme for Human
        Rights Education 38–9
USA
    cultural diversity 151
    foreign policy 82–3, 92, 154–5
    influence 19
    and IRA 150
    and Islamic world 41, 63, 66–7,
        82–3, 101
    Lewis' influence 62

McCarthyism 142–3, 163
    origins of the nation 150
    popular and gun culture 98
    reason for scientific and cultural
        advances 120
    and terrorism 141–2, 152
    tolerance and prejudices 90–1
Usque, Samuel 90

Vasic (Balkan journalist) 143–4
veiling 10–11
Versailles, Treaty of (1919) 43, 167
Vinaya Pitaka 81
Visva-Bharati University 123–4
Voltaire 51

Wahid, Abdurrahman 85, 168
Wang Xuezhen 109
Weil, Simone 138
West
    belief in own superiority 52, 55–9
    colonialism and imperialism
        27–8, 52–3, 55, 67, 153–6
    and Islamic world 41, 62–3, 66–9,
        82–3, 91, 101, 151–5
    massacres in Turkey 6
    things could teach Islam and vice
        versa 71
Wickramasinghe, Dr Chandra 75,
    168
women 10–12, 34, 38, 71
World War I see First World War
World War II see Second World
    War

xenophobia 68, 70, 87, 141–6, 152

Yalman, Nur
    appearance and interests ix–xi
    in Britain 74
    education 119–21
    speeches by 1, 141–56
Young Turks 36
Yugoslavia, former 69, 115, 143

Zhou Enlai 110
Ziya Pasha 36, 168
Zweig, Stefan 34, 168